MORE
EX CATHEDRAS

(XVI - XXII)

PETER JOANNIDES

Copyright © 2013 by Peter Joannides
All rights reserved.

This book or any portion thereof may not be reproduced or used in any manner whatsoever without the express written permission of the publisher except for the use of brief quotations in a book review.

Printed in the United States of America

Corrected second printing, 2019

ISBN 978-0-9892536-5-9

www.PetroulisI@gmail.com

PREFACE

The **Ex Cathedras** in this volume are part of a longer series begun in 1972 and continued to the present day (spanning over 41 years and totaling 23 installments). The first eight are embedded in my major work *Amán Amán!* (Amazon, 2013)—the initial three published in the Jacksonville University newspaper "The Navigator" and simply photographed with all mistakes and warts remaining as they were. (**Ex Cathedras 4** through **8**, however, were edited.)

When I completed *Amán Amán!* I never again wanted to involve myself in anything so painful as the sort of writing I had been doing. Every writing bout was like being led to an inquisition chamber. I knew I had created something of value, but I didn't want to go through any more agony. In addition, I felt I had accomplished what I set out to accomplish.

However, I did want to keep my hand in. My love of language, literature, and writing had not abated. And so I continued with the **Ex Cathedras**, writing one at a time with sometimes as many as four years separating one from the next, but usually about a year or two.

Writing the **Ex Cathedras** was not painful—just the reverse. I would simply wait until the thought occurred, and then record it. After which I would embellish, improve, adjust, try to perfect. Unlike the efforts with the Magnum Opus, this process was pleasurable and delightful.

Nearly all the **Ex Cathedras** were privately printed in the form of a small spiral-bound booklet, in which a page had to be turned for each entry. To duplicate this original form would no doubt be commercially prohibitive, and so in this volume, roughly four entries are included on each page.

It has become obvious to me in reviewing these past **Ex Cathedras** that there are many duplications and hardly disguised repetitions. I suppose I may owe the Reader an apology. However, it should be borne in mind that years would elapse from one **Ex Cathedra** to the next, I would forget, and certain themes were clearly and repeatedly occupying my mind more than others. Certainly these repetitions could have been editorially excised from the present book, but I wanted to be faithful to the originals and, more importantly, to the time and spirit of the moments I lived. Perhaps the best justification and defense is that each **Ex Cathedra** should be looked upon as an autonomous unit, and judged accordingly.

Some entries were minimally edited relative to the booklet originals.

Together with **Ex Cathedras IX–XV**, this volume completes the collection of **Ex Cathedras** written up to September 15, 2012.

Peter Joannides

CONTENTS

Ex Cathedra 16	1
Ex Cathedra 17	63
Ex Cathedra 18	123
Ex Cathedra 19	183
Ex Cathedra 20	245
Ex Cathedra 21	309
Ex Cathedra 22	371

May 1, 2006

Ex Cathedra

16th Encyclical

von Herrn Doktor Professor Peter Joannides

1

Life's too short to read the Sports Page.

2

There are all sorts of (human) wild animals out there. The thing to do is to try and keep out of their way.

3

Rap is shit.

4

Greek Rap:

Double Shit.

5

Nausea is a terrible thing.

If one had to suffer nausea for several hours a day, for the rest of his allotted days, Life would not be worth living.

6

The thought has often occurred to me. And invariably haunts me:

One's first love ought to be one's last.

7

It takes a courageous man to throw off the habits and brainwashing of a lifetime.

8

It seems to me that a benevolent planetary dictator would have as his first order of business the ample funding for research and development of methods to deflect an errant comet or asteroid bound for a collision with earth.

9

The destination of all pursuits and thrusts and yearnings toward a better, an ideal, a utopian world—whether it has to do with sex, social intercourse, intellectual stimulation, health, aesthetics, sport, gastronomy, pristine wilderness, friendship, literature, knowledge, loyalty, whatever—is to **M A T C H** the drinking of cool cool water when terribly terribly thirsty.

10

Just about always, it's either too hot or too cold.

Every once in a blue moon, it's just right.

11

All my life I've been so starved of the right company, I find myself making overtures to the wrong company.

12

I'm not very good with deadlines.

I'm much better with finish-the-project-no-matter-how-long-it-takes-lines.

13

Elli Stai: News Anchorwoman of the Greek "Antenna" Network.

Talk about **H U B R I S !**

14

I don't need critics, exegetes, pundits to explain what I've accomplished.

I know what I've accomplished.

15

If I had to be an expert on something, and we've already mentioned sex and color and wildflowers and liquor and liquor bottles,
then let it be cheeses.

16

This entry is strictly the property of L.W. Boothby, my old Fork Union buddy:

Reality is an illusion created by a lack of alcohol.

17

There is officially no such word as "exegesist."

There SHOULD be such a word. It flows naturally from "exegesis," has an appropriately pedantic-sounding ring, and is generally a much better candidate than "exegete."

18

A little bit of meat can take the place of a whole lot of vegetables.

19

It seems to me that a benevolent planetary dictator would have as his first order of business the ample funding for research and development of methods to prevent or neutralize an errant virus or microorganism that could decimate the human race.

20

Why Gore Vidal would want to take part in a Bill Maher show together with all those fluffy mouthing idiots is absolutely beyond me.

(Just as I was about to finally forgive him for **Mary Hartman, Mary Hartman**.)

I think perhaps there may be a major flaw in his character.

21

The P-40, the P-39 Airacobra were such good-looking, handsome airplanes!

22

There are no nationalities.

There are only psychological types that cut right across all nationalities.

23

Commencement speeches are mostly shit.

24

I've seen the heather in Scotland.

My life has not been lived in vain.

25

The "Borscht Belt" comedians may have been quick, sure-fire intelligent, very much "with it," "perfect timing," "razor-witty"…

But they were also vulgar.

26

Television:

Garbage everywhere.

There's garbage in the U.K., just as in the U.S.A.

Garbage garbage, everywhere.

27

You can't take a fragment of Joannides' work and say, "This is what he thinks."

What Joannides thinks is his Whole Book.

The Book, The Whole Book, and nothing but The Book.

28

I detest most American music.

29

How I love to be seated at a banquet table that is one-third empty and siphon all those extra goodies from my adjacent and non-existent tablemates.

30

When I get really sexually excited, the most outlandish, unbelievable depravities cross my mind.

31

If I see one more football (or soccer) game, I think I'll scream!

32

If mangoes did not exist, the Universe would be greatly diminished thereby.

33

Once you lie, how can one ever know that you're not lying again?

34

I've always wanted to have a meal with just starters.

And forget all about the main course.

35

Nothing gets my dander up quite like a chicken-shit cop.

36

When it is someone else who wins the Gigantic Lotto Prize, I get sick to my stomach.

37

I never did like piano solo.

38

A planet with a projected 30 billion inhabitants.

I want no part of it.

Just the thought of it makes me sick.

39

The fires have cooled.

I never thought that this would really happen.

40

I've never been comfortable with the word "venue."

I don't know what it really means, I don't know how to use it properly, I dare not have anything to do with it.

It is not **MY** word.

41

I just realized something significant about all my friends: I can't imagine a single one of them **DECLAIMING**.

42

How I wish I were like Prince Ibis and had his mysterious magical vibrating Ibstick.

43

Thank God for all those near-misses!

44

There's something about those who relish lecturing and displaying their wit to young captive audiences that is nothing less than sickening.

45

Torture has occurred.

Nothing can ever make up for it.

46

There are hooligans in every country, from Andorra to Botswana to Japan to Kyrgyzstan to Venezuela to Zanzibar.

You can't judge a country by its hooligans.

47

As with filet mignon, scallops can also be like a **lokoum**.

48

English is **NOT** the language for a Greek liturgy.

49

I can't tell you how much it disturbs me, were Jules Verne to suddenly and miraculously come back from the dead and I were to blissfully and swooningly show him around, not to have the scientific and technological expertise to properly explain all the new-found marvels.

50

I want to be the first Planetarch.

51

I want my work published so that I can criticize, qualify, adjust, disown, apologize for, insist upon, revise, explain, amplify, amend it.

52

Watching the History Channel is like going to school all over again.

53

Students are generally smarter than their professors.

54

I don't use chopsticks.

55

So much time has elapsed.

I don't know if my work is more like old and vintage wine, bettered and bettered and more precious with age.

Or like one Gigantic Anachronism.

56

If you look upon those who offend and distaste you as **animals**, a whole new landscape appears that is clearer, and a course of action made simpler.

57

There's a whole world out there—of scientists and engineers and mechanics and electricians and pipefitters—that humbles and intimidates me.

58

The world needs people who love and admire the work of Logan Pearsall Smith.

59

I don't mind arriving at a queue and finding bodies there ahead of me, already established.

But when someone beats me by literally half a second and then spends my time hemming and hawing and asking questions and doing his banking where there is not a bank and otherwise fumbling and dawdling,

I just want to scream, strangle, and bash his or her head in.

60

I want nothing less than to have my work fussed over, probed, annotated, analyzed, critiqued, concordanced, reviled, nit-picked, eulogized, apotheosized—

just like **Ulysses**.

61

"Bits and Pieces, Glimpses"

A wonderful title.

For all manner of contents.

62

It just boggles my mind that there are people who like to drink **after** dinner.

63

I am haunted and surrounded by dead people.

64

I don't dance minuets with women.

65

Fred Harris: Never have I known anyone so **AT ONE** with the American language.

(It is impossible for Fred Harris to make a mistake in American usage.)

66

I don't whistle "zippy-doo-da" anymore.

I know what's going on.

67

Installing electric-eye flushing toilets is really stupid.

68

I am beginning to hate ads. **ALL** ads.

69

I love to watch Derek Jeter play baseball.

70

Eating a good (triple-cream) brie is like getting quietly and beautifully drunk.

71

I read (past tense) what I read when I read it.

It's too late to read anymore.

72

The flaw in Ayn Rand is that she's preachy.

73

      Why people climb formidable and dangerous mountains, try to save Rwandan gorillas, madly race cars around a speedway, explore ocean depths for hitherto unknown biological species, inch their way up corporate ladders, be experts on frogs, gall-bladders, and periodontic disease, run for mayor, pump iron, monomaniacally pursue investments...

                                    when there's sex...

                                                        is a little difficult for me to understand.

74

      Half the time I don't know what analysts, economists, mechanics, doctors, lawyers, financiers, statisticians are talking about.

75

NO ANIMALS INDOORS!

76

Pursuing the theme of "If I had to be an expert on something, then let it be…," I think that after cheeses I would have to go with soups.

77

Every day the clackety-clackying of my car over the partitions and dividers of a roadway reminds of a train.

78

I love the way trains **slice through** things.

79

There is something especially piquant and delightsome about having sex with an especially intelligent woman.

80

There are all sorts of lists I can think of, where, at the very bottom of the barrel, would be Oliver North.

81

Sex is not the most important thing, but it seems to **obliterate** all that dares stand before it.

82

Ann Coulter: I wonder what rock she managed to crawl out from under.

83

A lot can be learned from good stand-up comedians.

84

I hate waiting in line for anything, but especially so for food.

85

Why is the word "irredressible / irredressable" found in the **OED** but nowhere in the **Unabridged Webster's**, **Random House**, or **American Heritage**?

86

It's getting to the point where, as soon as I see an ad, I want to vomit.

87

I miss Wayne. God, how I miss Wayne and his expertise.

88

Senator John Warner of Virginia is a pompous pretentious asshole.

I even like President Bush more than I do Senator John Warner of Virginia.

89

I'm still trying to figure out why soldiers obey orders and go to war.

90

There's no doubt about it: if you're going to be reincarnated, the best to be is an otter.

91

The best of the **Airport** films is the first one.

92

Sometimes you can garner quite a bit from a whiff.

And I've had many and wide and varied a whiff.

93

I have just finished reading Robert MacNeil's and William Cran's **Do You Speak American?**

On a descriptivist-prescriptivist scale of 1 to 10, if John Simon is a 10 and Jesse Sheidlower a 1, then William Safire is a 9, Robert S. Bryan a 9, I an 8, and Wayne Hamm a 7.

Wayne, a **NEAR GENIUS**, was a 7!

THAT JUST SAYS IT ALL.

94

Hopefully, the dangling "hopefully" will eventually be accepted by the academic purists and die-hards.

95

Bombarded and unwanted unasked-for "music" has been the bane of my existence.

96

I live out of the trunk of my car.

97

Whenever something halfway significant happens, the networks are ready to talk it to death.

98

The World unfolds as it must unfold, and couldn't have unfolded in any other way than the way it did unfold.

99

I guess it was a Golden Age when WKTZ Stereo 90.9 Radio would just play continuous soothing music without any solicitations.

100

I pretty much give everyone the benefit of the doubt.

But some are just beyond the pale.

101

I really like old friends.

I mean really old friends that go back a long long way.

102

British ladies employed on American TV and Radio ought to go home.

103

White chocolate is not chocolate.

104

Some people are easy on the eyes.

(And some aren't.)

105

I shall never forget that Easter night in Binghamton, New York in 1953 or 54, when Mama and I were trying to find the Greek church only to be mistakenly directed to the Russian one instead, at a little before midnight, and Mama saying we might as well stay as it would be fruitless to find the Greek one in time,

and to be suddenly immersed in the wonder and ambience of the ceremonies in this now exotic language of Russian.

Never before or since have I felt the spirit of Easter as I did that night with

Христос воскрес! Воистину Воскресе!

106

Wouldn't it be fascinating to meet a ravishing woman and not exchange any information about one another—not even first names—and to have the most outlandish, superlative, unparalleled sex—
and **THEN** to slowly discover all the details and niceties of one another.

107

Actually, I too am a specialist.

A specialist on being a generalist.

108

There are times, not all the time but there are times—when an American accent just grates on my nerves.

109

Just because there's more on the plate,

Doesn't mean you have to finish it.

110

I'm not at all sure that my opinions, outlooks, prejudices, persuasions at the age of 51 were not far more valid than the ones I have now.

111

George Carlin is vulgar.

(But he's a good and "right-on" vulgar.)

112

"Merde!" is a much better expression than "Shit!"

113

Sometimes I think I'm as good as any polygraph machine.

114

As far as I'm concerned, **Jerry Seinfeld** was always garbage.

115

The beauty of getting old is the enormous number of things you're free of and are no longer interested in.

116

How can so many be so smart and withal so retarded?

in Greece

117

The sound of male horseplay on the beach: a more disgusting barrage on the ear can hardly be imagined.

118

It's getting to the point that when I travel, I want to be met at the airport (seaport, station) by friends. I want to be shown around, shown the sights by friends. I want to be taken to the right restaurants (hotels) by friends, and explained, put up, catered to, smoothed over formalities, fees, visas, customs, exchange rates, restrictions, queries by friends.

No friends; no travel.

119

The Albanian flag is a manly flag.

120

Young actors trying to get ahead and make a name for themselves—make me sick.

Old actors that are still hanging on—make me sad.

121

I wish these precious doting dog-lovers would take their raspy, smelly, ugly freakeries and shove them up their ass.

122

There's just no way to get around it: Sex turns practically everyone into a Jekyll and Hyde.

123

One day neckties will be as quaint as fedoras.

124

Groupies, groupies everywhere: nude groupies, gay groupies, tourist groupies, academic groupies, sport groupies, political groupies, pet groupies, swinger groupies, religious groupies, collector groupies, business groupies, art groupies...

I reject the whole lot of them.

125

I guess Greeks **ARE** different from Turks.

It's the music that really says it all.

126

I can't stand that sweet and sickly, sweetness and slush and light, **Reader's Digest** quality.

127

"In" places are out for me.

128

The only one who understands all about me is me.

129

DJ's ply a disgusting trade, right up there with actors, politicians, tour guides, and career Army officers.

130

If I were running things, mufflerless motorcyclists would not only be immediately arrested and thrown in the darkest prison, but also given extra hard labor, solitary confinement, and 30 lashes.

131

As the perceptive and faithful Reader of my **Ex Cathedras** will have already surmised, a visit to Greece resurrects the same old themes.

And so, on pain of repetition:

Why can't there be a radio station in Greece that just plays Greek music, on and on forever on beautiful and exquisite Greek music, no interruptions, no cute and oily ads, no political analyses, no news items, no slimy DJ's, no shitty American screechings suddenly following a wondrous Greek song (like a sacrilegious ice-cold shower), no station identification, no goddam **TALK!**

Just Greek music, on and on forever on beautiful and exquisite Greek music.

132

I hope all mufflerless motorcyclists die!

133

The world is full of peasants.

134

The world of "canned":

Canned music, canned song, canned dance, canned revelries, canned tours, canned ceremonies, canned interviews, canned worship, canned classrooms, canned souls.

135

I'm no great friend of watermelon, unless it's very very very cold, and very very very good.

136

If I had to rank the literary and philosophical titans and geniuses of our time, I think it would have to go something like this: first, Logan Pearsall Smith, then F. Nietzsche, then Thomas Wolfe, then F. Dostoyevsky, then H.G. Wells, and finally Ludwig Wittgenstein.

137

Day by day, every day, all I see around me are types. Hardly ever an original.

138

Memory distills.

If only one could experience the distillation **in the very happening**. But too many annoyances and distractions: excessive heat, cold, noise, hunger, thirst, blinding sunlight, necessary needs and functions, interruptions, aches and pains, timetables, chit-chat, nags, worries.

139

The philosopher's task: to put together the whole jig-saw puzzle from the few bits and pieces thrown his way.

140

Little fish are ferocious fish for littler fish.

141

I love the crisp "t's" of British speech.

142

Another hilarious Greek-American translation gem:

"We ate Rhodos with a spoon."

back home

143

I don't care what his knowledge, erudition, writing skills, insights, talents may have been, I never did and still don't like Edmund Wilson.

144

All these upstarts and academic shits—Kaufmann, Birx—intent on "revising" and "updating" the original and wondrous Thomas Common translation of **Zarathustra**.

145

I wonder if others are as nasty as I am in my under-my-breath mutterings.

146

Soldiers should tell their governments to go stick it up their ass.

147

I wonder if Maxwell Perkins, being the perspicacious editor that he was, realized that Wolfe was head and shoulders above Fitzgerald, Hemingway, Rawlings, et al.

148

Oh how often I think of Wolfe's credo in **You Can't Go Home Again** where the enemy comes in the guise of a friend.

149

Chicken livers prepared by **i makarítisa** Anita Magat: unparalleled, heavenly, supernal!

150

Whenever someone else wins the Gigantic Lotto Prize, it takes me several days to get over it.

151

Overrated:

Einstein, James Joyce, William Faulkner, Marlon Brando, Winston Churchill, St. Thomas Aquinas, Plato, Ingmar Bergman, Isaiah Berlin, Lawrence Olivier, Will Rogers, Mortimer Adler.

Underrated:

Logan Pearsall Smith, Max Beerbohm, Jules Verne, Thomas Wolfe, Andy Rooney, Robert Benchley, Eugene Debs, Robert Owen, Ambrose Bierce, James Cagney, Lafcadio Hearn, Sid Caesar, Rex Stout.

152

Arthur C. Clarke's Duplicator Machines: the ultimate in technology:

Anything into Anything.

153

Oh what I wouldn't give to somehow somewhere sometime find my alter ego!

154

I feel this terrible obligation to all sorts of dead people.

155

I think I dislike Bill Frist and Tom DeLay **EACH** more than I do Bush, Phil Gramm, Trent Lott, and John Warner **COMBINED**.

156

All these national demigods—Kemal, Marti, Venizelos, Lincoln, Bolivar—I wonder how demigoddic they really were.

157

Colors seen when ruminating about them philosophically are quite different from colors seen everyday normally.

158

All are inferior.

Only Nietzsche is not inferior.

159

Sometimes I **SCREAM** at ornery, uncooperative, deliberately malicious, disappearing, in-the-furthest-remotest-crack-lodging inanimate objects.

160

Some things are true, but just can't be said in language: solipsism, determinism, sense-dataism, egoism.

161

Three of the ugliest accents on this planet: Brooklyn, Texas Drawl, and Diana-Rigg-Upper-Pretentious-British.

162

There are more bad doctors than good ones.

163

The problems of pain need to be addressed before the problems of pleasure.

164

Little did we know as children what a much wider world there was out there.

165

What a phony stance, this encyclopaedic presumption that there is a common fund of knowledge that any educated person is privy to.

The fact is that every day I learn about things and people I never heard of before (although common knowledge for those specializing), every day full of newnesses and surprises.

Like a never-receding fog.

166

I envy no man on earth.

Except one who is exactly like me, but has a great deal of money.

167

Actually, most politicos are too stupid to be diabolical.

168

Gay sex: I just like the nastiness of it.

(And its almost effortless availability.)

169

The Elements of Style by E.B. White and William Strunk: that Anglo-Saxon paragon of clarity and succinctness and sheer good sense.

The older I get, the more insidious I think that little book is.

170

Maybe, after all, that **IS** the way it is:

"The Ghost in the Machine."

171

Reincarnation?

Oh God! I don't want to go through it again.

172

Since I have such a terribly low tolerance for pain,

I can identify with **ALL** who are in pain.

173

Just think about it: how essentially different **1984** was from 1984.

So much to be said for prophets, prognosticators, seers, forecasters, and assorted self-proclaimed intellectuals.

174

Goodness and kindness supersede everything.

175

India:

How can a people who eat such awful food produce such poignant and soul-clasping music?

176

 I hope I never again am beholden to another obligation, of **whatever** sort, at 8:00 o' clock in the morning.

177

 Oh how cocky and cocksure I was not so many years ago!

178

 I absolutely refuse to watch any dramatization of a Jules Verne book.

 Or one involving Nero Wolfe.

179

Pure Bliss:

Breakfast at the Waffle House around 11A.M., after a thorough workout and swim at the Y:

Waffle topped with butter and rivulets of syrup, extra-soft scrambled eggs, three strips of extra crisp and crinkly bacon, grits covered with butter, sugar, and a dollop of milk, raisin toast accompanied by apple-butter jam.

180

It just fascinates me:

With what **ZEAL** all these experts and authorities latch on to their respective fragments.

181

Life:

A certain surface scum found on certain minor planets.

What an exhilarating thought!

182

This is a world of e-mails; it is no longer a world of letters.

Lament it how you will, it is no longer a world of letters.

183

There is a certain purity about good pornography that cannot be gainsaid.

184

I can smell a Republican from a considerable distance.

185

After a repast I want to go directly to bed.

No chit-chat, no clean-up, no transport, no constitutional, no dilly-dallying—just straight to bed.

186

What good is sex without a story line.

187

I've said it before, and I say it again:

Nothing bores me more than football philosophers.

188

Real history begins with photographs.

Before that it's all a matter of projection, nebulousness, conjecture, and surmise.

189

Should I win the lottery, not at all interested in pursuing: yachts, private Lear jets, jewelry, 45-room 18-bathroom mansions, parties for 5000 of my closest friends, Rolex watches, priceless art treasures, Gucci creations, Armani creations, celebrities, Rolls Royces - Ferraris - Mercedes Benz SLR's, Manhattan penthouse apartments, servants, knighthoods, country clubs.

Interested in pursuing: lobster tails, the finest restaurants, the finest wines and spirits, 5-star hotels, the classiest call girls, the remotest islands and wildest inaccessible places, pristine beaches, padding bank accounts of friends, massages, learning languages, being psychoanalyzed by a first-rate psychoanalyst (hard to find amongst so many charlatans and frauds), sampling all the drugs and opiates (under medical supervision), stone crabs.

190

I keep forgetting how much redneck crud there abides in Jacksonville.

191

Convalescing is sweet.

192

I don't want to have to think about money.

I don't want to have to think about the workings and misworkings of my body.

I don't want to have to think about cooking, shopping, laundry, taking out the garbage, washing dishes, raking leaves, paying bills, punching clocks, waiting in line, filing tax returns, attending ceremonies...

I have other things to do.

193

Goodbye, goodbye to all that: circuses, parades, Disneylands, crowds, lectures, seminars, speeches, committees, concerts, theaters, fairs, ceremonies, parties, tours, cruises, stadiums, marches, monuments...

194

The opening ceremonies of the XX Winter Olympic Games, Torino, Italy:

` Halfway tasteful and dignified as the proceedings were, that little bit of fluff (Yoko Ono and homilies about peace along with the usual hippie musical wailings) just had to work itself in.

195

Pure Bliss:

A Dubonnet, under a warm and caressing sunlight, with a good cigar.

196

The closing ceremonies of the XX Winter Olympic Games, Torino, Italy:

Ricky Martin and co.: pure unadulterated shit.

197

American/Caribbean music

No matter how sometime similar they are, that little bit of difference MAKES (HEAVEN BE PRAISED!) ALL THE DIFFERENCE.

198

Updated list of those that I cannot bear watching for more than five seconds (at the outside): O'Reilly, Woody Allen, Bill Frist, Tom DeLay, Bill Cosby, Bryant Gumbel, Karen Hughes, John Travolta, Chris Rock, Chuck Norris, Mr. Rogers, Dr. Phil, Donald Trump, Phil Gramm, Nancy Grace, Richard Branson, Dennis Miller, Dr. Laura Schlessinger.

199

There's something a bit discomfiting about Black Republicans.

200

I do not send SASE's, nor do I talk to machines.

201

The contours of a woman: the slightest over- under-compensation makes so so much difference.

202

One must be somewhat of an idiot not to see the essential and uninterrupted kinship of humans and animals.

203

One must be somewhat of an idiot to believe in a Benevolent God in light of accidents, illnesses, pandemics, earthquakes, and floods.

May 13, 2007

Ex Cathedra

17th Encyclical

von Herrn Doktor Professor Peter Joannides

1

Small talk is ofttimes necessary before big talk.

2

Women in Arab garb, IN THE STATES, really turn me off.

3

The most irritating thing about Americans is their love of dogs.

4

Sweet and tender love—yes.

Sweet and tender sex: an oxymoron.

5

I get very nervous around crazies.

6

I drink and drive all the time.

But when doing so I observe all the rules and regulations TO THE LETTER.

7

Oriana Fallaci:

I probably would not have agreed with all she professed, but I suspect I would have liked and respected her enormously.

8

I can no longer do things that don't agree with me.

9

    Tête-à-tête communicating with animals: misplaced loyalty and saccharoid empathy.

10

    The sound of a basketball aimlessly dribbled can drive me insane.

11

    If one is to assign a definite date for the Big Bang, I have every right to ask what went on before that date.

12

    I murderously resent hard-to-open pistachios.

13

The word "patrician" simply does not apply to Americans.

in Greece

14

The stories of Jhumpa Lahiri:

Original and exquisite artistry of gloom and doom, cast in a modern Indian-American setting, reminiscent of both Simenon and Thomas Hardy.

15

Greeks:

Of all nationalities, the loudest beach-goers.

Whose inane prattle can waft and bombard for nearly half a mile.

16

Whenever I think that there are others who think and feel and experience differently than I, and that therefore solipsism is false, it inevitably occurs to me that it is always **I** who think that they think differently, it is always **I** who imagines what it would be like for them to feel and experience differently, **I** who always empathizes and projects, **I** who puts myself in their place, **I** who entertains and defines this very notion of otherness.

Solipsism is true.

17

It's terrible to not be awed by hardly anything anymore.

18

Some are so cheap and coarse and vulgar, there simply is no communication—not even anti-communication.

19

There is so much riff-raff in this world.

20

Lackeys and Disgust

Like the North Korean generals eagerly clapping their hands as they dutifully trot behind Dear Leader Kim Jong Il.

21

Lambros Kostandaras: a wonderful Greek actor.

22

I find myself saying "Fuck you!" and "Shit!" at least 20 times a day.

To all sorts of deserving subjects.

23

Of all professions, that of a compassionate, able, and assiduous nurse has to be the highest in the eyes of God.

24

Nudist Beach in Rhodos

Most of the women look like cows, a few are passable but imperfect, another few nubile and slender and interesting, and a very very few look like Varga Girls.

25

Soccer is one gigantic bore.

26

For those familiar with my work, there is a woman in Athens (a professional woman) even more beautiful than that Eurasian girl I espied so many years ago in Hong Kong.

She almost literally takes my breath away.

27

    I just can't get away from it—the lousy American music—no matter how hard I try—loudspeakers and wires in restaurants, taxis, patios, hallways, emporiums, discos—blaring and offending—spoiling obliterating cheapening—all over the world.

28

    Patrick Leigh Fermor: still going strong.

    But he must have dug deep in the **OED** to find words to use that nobody uses.

29

    It would pain me greatly were I to learn that Lambros Kostandaras had in real life been brusque and insensitive.

30

Greek ads and solicitations are as vomit-producing as American ones—perhaps even more so.

But Miami-Spanish ones are still the worst of all.

31

I simply don't like stairs anymore. They're slowly becoming menacing and formidable enemies.

32

Greek clergy with their black robes and flowing beards and golden scepters and top hats and gargoyle voices are getting ridiculouser and ridiculouser, day by day.

33

Lots of political windbags in Greece.

34

Should I ever become The Planetary Dictator, there's no question that I would have a harem.

35

What my friends don't realize when they question the point of my seeking an alter ego,

Is that my alter ego will be very very much like me, but not exactly like me.

36

Desecrations and graffiti on trains in large cities depress me deeply.

37

When I'm away from America, I like to be away from Americans.

back home

38

Unless it's really really good company, I more and more prefer my own company.

39

Very very very few people should have handguns.

40

"What if I had been born a zebra?"

What I wouldn't give for Wittgenstein to analyze this supposition.

41

No one better fits the bill of (in old New York days) a "**tsifoútis**" than a) Larry King and b) Woody Allen.

42

I really couldn't care less what the man in the street thinks—about anything.

43

John Updike:

That encyclopaedic and all-knowing afflatus of his is just too much!

44

I not only have prejudices; I flaunt my prejudices.

45

I prefer words over numbers.

46

Once, for a few lost moments or one brief instant, our paths did cross: Frank Sinatra, Lilly Palmer, Wilbur Mills, John Dos Passos, Rod Steiger, Haile Selassie, Omar Sharif, Hermann Hesse, Telly Savalas, Henry Miller, Charles Bronson, King Hassan II, J.D. Salinger, Isaac Asimov, The Dalai Lama, Stephen Spender, Dana Andrews, Archbishop Makarios, Walter Cronkite.

47

Really square, straight-laced, church-going, eye-blinkered, pitchfork-couple people—do have some virtues.

48

Some doctors are just slimes.

49

There is no exact English equivalent for the Greek word "**trómaksa**." The only way is a sort of circumlocution: "I was suddenly startled/terrified."

(Sort of like "**simbethéra**"="the mother of my daughter-(son)-in-law.")

((They tell me that Eskimos have twenty different words for "snow."))

50

The Ultimate Drug:

That which would take me back to an early time—to long-lost experiences in all their specificness and immediacy—and still empower me to be my present me.

Worth all the crack, cocaine, weed, mescaline, LSD, heroin, Demerol, and alcohol put together.

51

I can't bear fiction anymore. Whether in the form of novels, films, short stories, dramas, what have you (all except porno).

I hunt for documentaries.

52

It's a great advantage to be anonymous.

53

Not very profound, tasteful, or effective critics: Michael Moore, Al Franken.

54

Ann Coulter: one sick lady!

55

I guess one of these days, sooner or later, I'm going to have to accept "very unique."

56

In my last **Ex Cathedra** I had an entry on groupies. All sorts of groupie groupies.

I forgot to include literary groupies.

57

I love heavy rain.

It turns me into an instant philosopher.

58

Cardinal Richelieu's astute and discerning awareness:

Kittens and cats are two different orders of being.

59

    Defacing and hard-to-peel-off logos and price tags pasted onto individual pieces of fruit or vegetable—

    Infuriate me.

60

    Can water be delicious?

61

    Odor can be dulcet and voluptuous and the doorway to haunting and indistinct bygone wisps…

    and it can also bludgeon you.

62

    I don't like ads, nor do I like people who do ads.

63

I'll take Castro over Batista anytime.

64

Pierced and ringed earlobes, tongues, nipples, bellybuttons, penises, labia—what a disgusting practice!

65

Isn't it interesting, as one acquires a taste for retsina, that what starts out as kerosene/turpentine ends up as life-giving nectar.

66

Thank God for Americans who don't have bumper stickers on their cars.

67

I only like books where every word was written, and every revision made, by the author himself.

68

I like to be with people who don't have to work for a living.

69

A wonderful line by Andy Rooney: "Milk without fat is like non-alcoholic Scotch."

70

The other day at Piccadilly Cafeteria I saw a young lady on her cell phone throughout her whole meal, beginning to end. Dining with one hand and ear-pressed with the other. As she got up to pay her bill, still on her cell phone.

Can you imagine anyone having such disrespect for food?

71

There are no highborn Americans.

All Americans, of necessity and circumstance, are lowborn.

72

I agree with Andy Rooney 90% of the time.

73

In a debate, I'd probably be a disaster.

But I'm still smarter.

74

I like Frank Capra, and I like all the movies of Frank Capra.

75

If someplace is "HISTORIC," it must simply BE so.

It is most gauche and self-preening for it to proclaim itself so.

76

Voting is essentially an irrational act.

(But it would be less than wise for this to be broadcast or disseminated.)

77

I've lost touch with so many, so many.

I'VE NEVER WANTED TO LOSE TOUCH WITH ANYBODY.

78

The emptier the stomach, the greater the alcoholic epiphany.

79

Imagine a heightened literary awareness combined with a heightened philosophic awareness combined with a heightened scientific awareness.

80

Pursuant to **Entry 71**:

It takes more than two or three generations to form a genuine aristocracy.

81

Death is so Other that it isn't even other.

82

I can't stand swimmers who do up and down uninterrupted laps in a pool. Up and down, up and down (count them asshole!), like a fucking mindless machine.

I just can't stand them.

83

Those final lines of **Zarathustra**. I think at last I understand.

" '**Fellow suffering! Fellow suffering with the higher men!**' he cried out, and his countenance changed into brass. 'Well! **That**—hath had its time!' "

84

What is quintessentially American?

Archie Goodwin's accounts of the exploits of Nero Wolfe.

85

I've said it before, I don't remember when, but I say it again:

When actors philosophize, something rancid sets in.

86

I sometimes think about this:

Even O'Reilly was once a wide-eyed wondered child.

87

It's difficult for me to get much interested in any one thing, having for as long as I can remember this compelling interest in the all of things.

88

I'd rather miss the information than have it droned and spieled to me by a tour guide.

89

I've finally come up with the one word that captures the essence of the English: brittle.

90

Rum is to Scotch what Brazil is to Alaska.

91

Old friends are dying off, one after another, left and right.

92

To be truly eccentric, one has to be rich.

93

All these geographical name-changings: Beijing for Pekin, Myanmar for Burma, Sri Lanka for Ceylon, Kolkata for Calcutta, Mumbai for Bombay, Benin for Dahomey, Burkina Faso for Upper Volta, Iran for Persia, Thailand for Siam...

I prefer the old names.

94

Porno:

The more XXXX-rated, the better.

95

I feel this terrible and sacred obligation to all the Purities.

To **match** all the Purities.

96

When dining, I don't look forward to having a tray on my lap or settling into a booth. I'd much rather have **A TABLE AND A CHAIR**.

97

When blocked, go around.

98

No speech should ever last more than 15 minutes.

99

The fact is, solipsism is true of course.

For all of us.

100

There are friendly folk in Alaska, but there are no aristocrats in Alaska.

101

Chasing after sprites and vaporescent wisps and phantoms may be the highest calling.

102

You can deny it, you can qualify it, you can more or less try to get around it, but the fact is we've all (the whole planet, that is) been living under a Pax Americana for quite some time.

103

What is it about a rehearsal that invalidates the performance?

104

　　　　　Sometimes I want to **DIVE** into the books of Jules Verne...
　　　　　and never return.

105

No matter how good something is, after a while I want something else.

106

　　Internets, Downloadings, BlackBerries, Attachments, Modems… I've been left far behind.

107

Tyrone Power: the sweetest man on film I've ever seen.

108

　　I love the seriousness and dignity and tastefulness and probity of a BBC production.

109

　　Unattached papers and solicitations that come fluttering out of newly-bought magazines—

　　　　Infuriate me.

110

The loss of anonymity sometimes destroys the delight of sexual perversity.

111

There is no greater **cleanliness** than Jules Verne.

112

All who appear on panels, talk shows, conferences, colloquia, interviews are, no matter how old, adolescents.

113

Eulogies are generally uncomfortable, a little embarrassing, and wearily monochromatic.

114

What good is it to make money if it takes vanloads of time, drudgery, repetition, and weariness to do so.

115

John Edwards: No one who talks like that should have the temerity to run for President.

116

Southern Accents

First, let it be said that with respect to women, there is no problem.
With respect to men, however, it is another matter.
The accents of:

Joseph Cotten: positively take to.
Jimmy Carter, Shelby Foote, Sam Nunn: can come to terms with and take in stride.
Lyndon Johnson, James Baker, John Connally, Trent Lott: beginning to dislike.
John Edwards, Howard Baker, Ernest Hollings, Pat Robertson: dislike.
The pig-gruntings of Phil Gramm: positively abhor.

117

I'm sure that crocodiles probably look handsome to one another.

118

Silvio Berlusconi:

Corrupt, deceitful, two-faced, a little bit slimy.
(Although probably a good **compare** and drinking partner.)

This assessment is based not on evidence, but on first impression and cultivated instinct.

119

I hate Sundays. I've always hated Sundays.

Sundays are like Death.

120

Lately I've been thinking of Louis Hayward:

Light and aery and bantering and sophisticated, with a charming and delightful accent.

121

I've no great desire to go to Machu Picchu, Udaipur, Stratford-on-Avon, Capri, Prague, Warsaw; and none whatever to the French Riviera.

I'd love to go to Nouakchott, Bamako, Torres del Paine, Manaus, Limnos, Laccadives, Seychelles, Madeira, Darwin, and Thimbu.

122

There is nothing wrong with lots of fallen leaves left on a lawn.

123

What bad luck!—To have been born a Royal.

124

I still love to travel—**MY HIGHEST PASSION**—but now I want to do it comfortably.

125

I seem to be suddenly molting—skin after skin, bent after bent—at a rapid pace.

I wonder what I'm turning into.

126

The Razor's Edge

In its own oblique and suggestive and perhaps oversimplified way, it still was a memorable film.

127

Lately, I've been thinking:

Maybe Johnny Cash, William F. Buckley, Jr., John Leonard, Lewis Lapham, et al weren't really as bad as all that.

128

I'd like to take those singers who jazz up the old tried and true songs and hang them from the rafters by their balls and labia.

129

There is no such thing as an exceptional political luminary.

Anyone who would subject himself to the buffoonery, duplicity, and garbage of a political process is **ipso facto** an inferior being.

(The same considerations, **mutatis mutandis**, apply to actors.)

130

The other day I met an 82-yr old man who beamingly told me that during his whole lifetime he had only once had an alcoholic encounter—a thimbleful of beer—just to see what the taste was like.

He was quite proud of his accomplishment.

His justification had something to do with the **Bible**.

There went a very sick and pathetic old man.

131

Loud noises can drive me, an otherwise fairly easy-going and not unkind individual, **BERSERK!**

132

Cars hurtling down the Interstate at 75-80 mph capable of causing havoc should there be a tragic inadvertence...

Cars crawling along the Interstate seen from the window of an airplane (as in the General Motors Futurama at the 1939 New York World's Fair) like little ladybugs slowly and peacefully inching their way over cloverleafs and bantam thoroughfares...

Which is the true perception?

133

What can I do? I can't help who I don't like.

134

Thomas Sowell: there's a real doozy of a hubristic, pretentious, smug, self-important know-it-all.

(How **proud** he is to be the unusual black right-wing conservative spokesman.)

101

135

In a totally **laissez faire** society, what is to prevent one adroit, persistent, manipulative, and gifted individual from in the end legally owning everything?

(Might be a good idea for a movie.)

136

I continually get **eviscerated**. By a documentary, a eulogy, a forceful personality, an impassioned plea, a sentimentality, a polemic, an artistry, a zealotry…

But I soon get uneviscerated—and get back to my normal, critical self.

137

A truism: It is less painful to pay by credit card than by cash.

138

For a Compleat Hedonist, a chronic ailment involving even a minimal but annoying physical pain is a big matter.

139

Vanilla can't hack it next to chocolate.

140

Sometimes I want to **DIVE** into my beloved Greek music… and never return.

141

I judge people instantly and without reasons.

142

If I had to pick an individual whom I most admire, I guess Charles Darwin would not be a bad choice.

143

Professor Cornel West of Princeton University: Would make a good witchdoctor in an old Tarzan movie.

144

Jazz just doesn't do it for me. And never has.

145

I don't understand judges and lawyers.

I just can't follow their reasonings.

It's all too convoluted-intricate-twisted-regurgitated-enmeshed-entangled-ensnarled-incestuous-pedantic-doublespeak for me.

146

Some humans might as well be wild animals.

147

I know I've said it before, but I say it again:

(Repetition is not a bugaboo for me.)

I either want to run this planet.

Or be left alone to have a good time.

148

Sometimes the best (and sometimes the **only** good) thing about a contemporary fictional film is the technology depicted.

149

Most humans might as well be domestic animals.

150

Every day should be a renewal.

151

It's a great sin to go through life unmindful of the aesthetic dimension of things.

152

As soon as I win the lottery, I shall go to Nouakchott, Bamako, Torres del Paine, Manaus, Limnos, Laccadives, Seychelles, Madeira, Darwin, and Thimbu…**IN THAT ORDER**.

As well as fulfill a previous itinerary—a farm in Iowa, the bars and shantytowns of Barranquilla, a little village in Austria, the traffic snarls of Tokyo, a Hudson Bay station somewhere in the Northwest Territories, Lake Titicaca, a peasant village in the Ukraine, the middle of San Francisco, the Great Barrier Reef of Australia, masses of Indians bathing in the Ganges, the Underground of Atlanta, Molokai Island, a little village in Scotland, East Harlem in New York, a wandering tribe in Chad, somewhere deep in the Amazonas, Unimak Island in Alaska, masses and masses in Djakarta, a little town in Vermont…again, **IN THAT ORDER**.

153

I'm beginning to think sports are a bore.

154

Lately, when I have a little too much to drink—when a bit tipsy—I invariably lapse into a kind of nonsense German or into the few German expressions I am familiar with, repeating them over and over and over again:

Spieglein, Spieglein an der Wand, wer ist die Schönste im ganzen Land; Die Welt von Gestern; Du bist ein Esel mit meter langen Ohren; Die Aufgabe; Wo bist du?; Kennst du das Land, wo die Zitronen blühn…;Die Welt is alles, was der Fall ist; links-rechts-geradeaus.

I wonder why. Maybe it's just that German somehow tickles me. Or maybe some Super-Psychoanalyst can come up with a more involved explanation.

155

A population of 6,000,000,000 for this planet is nothing less than an obscenity.

156

I can't stand a documentary in which the focus is on those making the documentary rather than on what the documentary is supposedly about.

157

Except for a glass of cool cool water when terribly terribly thirsty, sex **AT ITS BEST** is the best thing there is.

158

The Economist, The New York Review of Books, National Geographic, Smithsonian, Scientific American, People Magazine, The Wall Street Journal, The New Yorker, Forbes, Sports Illustrated...

There isn't a person who knows anything more than a scantling, an infinitesimal scantling, of all that's going on in this world.

159

I've never really met anyone like me.

160

Beware of snap judgments, for you may be in for some rude surprises.

161

Loud and deafening music, however inspired and in-the-throes and gloriously ethnic, just gives me a headache.

162

There are so many things wrong with my body, I don't know which to complain about first.

163

When someone asks me to "hold on" on the telephone, I hold on for absolutely no longer than 2.5 minutes.

164

Europe = Clutter

165

What sort of creep would put a bumper sticker on the back of his car announcing:

"I ♥ MY WIFE"

166

There's something about a patriot that doesn't sit well with me.

167

I still feel a bit intimidated by those who speak French.

168

I wish you'd stop worrying about not mastering French.

Its heyday and hegemony are over.

Be thankful you speak the **current** planetary language.

169

Whenever I'm really hungry and have a pinkish-red medium-rare steak, I invariably think of the lions being fed at the zoo.

170

I keep my distance and get not an inch closer than 100 feet from all large animals.

And that includes dogs, horses, cattle, elephants, jackasses, and mules.

171

In the last year or so, it has dawned on me that I write, and always have written, for the healthy.

And not for the maimed, blind, deaf, retarded, severely ill, disfigured, and entrapped.

This is a humbling and poignant realization.

172

SHIBBOLETHS:

…for our children and our grandchildren…

…sends a message…

…The Founding Fathers…

…The American Dream…

…the bottom line…

…democracy…

…the American people…

…at this point in time…

…our American values…

…our community…

173

There is roughly one billionaire for every 6,000,000 inhabitants on this planet.

I wonder what the ratio is for one Walt Whitman.

174

Audio/pictorial history is better than written history.

175

Dessert shouldn't be had **after** dinner, but **with** dinner.

The contrast of sweet/non-sweet is delightful.

176

I sometimes wonder whether Wolfe and I might not have some DNA in common.

177

There are lottery winners.

And then there are lottery-in-reverse winners.

178

Determinism is as true as astrology is false.

179

There is no more grappling and vice-like hold than an obligation to the dead.

180

I'm so liberal, I'm conservative.

181

Oh these screaming shrieking screeching female American singers—these self-inflated, yawping "artists" and "entertainers"!

182

I wish that **I** could think up some of those jokes in **The New Yorker**.

183

There really are no conspiracies, power-elites, machinations, overlords…

There are only lost and bewildered souls throughout.

184

Of course there are exceptions, but undependability seems to generally be a Greek trait.

185

The first five inductees into my harem should I become the Planetary Dictator:

Head of Household: Maria Houkli.
Page Langton, Jenna Jameson, Catherine Zeta-Jones, Bonnie Schneider.

186

The first time for an ad or solicitation: can be interesting, clever, amusing.

The second time: a tinge of weariness starts to develop.

The third time: vomit begins to set in.

187

Nature programs and athletic events should be narrated by a **MALE**.

188

Thank God, Thank God for wildflowers, blue skies, sunlight, Jules Verne, Thomas Wolfe, F. Nietzsche, H.G. Wells, Logan Pearsall Smith, Robert Benchley, Rex Stout, rain forests, semi-deserts, **crème caramel**, **arní psitó me patátes**, "The Waiter and the Porter and the Upstairs Maid," "Music Makes Me," "**Bárba Iánni**," "Elmer's Tune," childhood memories, nasty sex, **ayióklima**, travel, love-at-first-sight, blackberries, raspberries, Dostoyevsky, Walt Whitman, handball, river deltas, "**Áma Thes na Fíyis, Fíye; Áma Thes na Klápsis, Klápse**," magazines, St. Francis of Assisi, **Karaghiózi**, Arctic and Antarctic Regions, maps, Carlo Buti, Carlos Gardel, **zeibékiko**, The Statue of Liberty, The Empire State Building, Ann Sothern, Cair retsina, The Staten Island Ferry…

189

Writers' Conferences, Writers' "Workshops": This has to be one of the most incestuous and insipid things I've ever heard about.

190

It's getting to the point where it's just too much trouble to get involved in a confrontation.

191

The care and solicitude of a nurse is the province of a **FEMALE**.

192

John Updike: his two cents are **EVERYWHERE**.

193

Oh from an author's written article, how obvious at times the airs and hubris and preening and pomposity of the author!

Ditto for the spoken word.

194

Ted Koppel: a really smart guy.

(But perhaps a wee bit too smart.)

195

A paradox: Here I am knowing next to nothing about economics, finance, science, engineering, medicine, physiology, mathematics, statistics, history (especially before 1850), music, art, politics, government, technology...
(I am not proud of such ignorance and feel somewhat embarrassed by it, especially with regard to science, engineering, and medicine.)

I have no idea how a car works, how a radio works, a cell phone, a television, an electric current, an airplane, an X-ray, a magnet, a sonogram...

I know precious little about wines, gastronomy, theater, opera, sculpture, poetry, fashion...

And yet I still feel superior.

196

Even if I were to win the Multimillion Dollar Lottery, I would still drive a Toyota Camry. (Or just maybe a Lexus 350.)

197

Some pursuits of the Planetary Dictator:

Destroy all nuclear bombs and nuclear-bomb capacities.
Destroy all biological and chemical arsenals (including the remaining laboratory specimens of smallpox).
Put the Amazon rain forest under quarantine.
Establish a gigantic Medical Research Center.
Establish a gigantic Pain Control Research Center.
Establish a significant Asteroid Collision Avoidance Center.
Squelch the Mafia.
Restrict and reverse population growth—with a long-term goal of 300,000,000.
Initiate the 3-hour work day, 3-day work week, 3-week work month, 3-month work year.

(continued)

198

Appoint a Scandinavian Czar for the Middle East—and woe to anyone who counters his edicts.
Appoint a Scandinavian Czar for Africa—and ditto.
Mete severe penalties for torturers, murderers, thieves, and scoundrels.
Establish an International Police Force—under the direct supervision of the Dictator's Scandinavian appointee(s).
Accept the annual tribute of three maidens from each sovereign country.
Tend to his harem, and to his culinary, aesthetic, philosophic, and literary explorations.

199

I suspect the Bible is probably a second-rate book.

Maybe even third-rate.

200

Road Maintenance in Jacksonville has shown me nothing but shit.

Ever since I got here in 1967.

October 15, 2008

Ex Cathedra

18th Encyclical

von Herrn Doktor Professor Peter Joannides

1

Richard Dawkins is right, of course.

But why belabor the obvious?

2

I always liked Jack Carson.

3

George Tobias

Ever since I was a teen-ager, I always thought George Tobias was a Greek-American. Because of the surname, I simply **assumed** he was of Greek background. I never questioned it. Never any independent corroboration. I have even on many occasions proudly proclaimed it to others: one of our earliest Greek-American actors.

Imagine then the shock of learning the other day that it isn't so. An apodeictic truth suddenly shattered. This is a devastating blow to me, and another learning experience—on a par with the "sunglasses episode" these many years ago in Santiago, Chile.

4

Cucumber is worthless, except as an adjunct to **oúzo**.

5

What I love about the lottery is the money given without any strings attached.

6

Bill Moyers

A first-rate lightweight.

7

Jonathan Miller

A highly intelligent and personable individual.

(And a hilarious mimicker of Oxford philosophers.)

8

I can pretty much tell a jerk from a mile away.

9

I'd love to have sex with Professor Lisa Randall of Harvard University.

10

Some celebrities are just plain physically **repellent**, aside from their opinions, mannerisms, accents, diction, etc. I dare not mention names, as that wouldn't be nice, given their total unresponsibility for their bodies.

But there it is: just plain **physically repellent**.

11

Superintendent of Schools: What an insipid, intrigue-laden, cliché-ridden, pasty vapid job.

12

The greatest sneak-up-on-you drink of all: **caipirinha**.

13

Mitt Romney: He looks like he just came out of a wax museum.

14

What greater clone than a large international airport.

15

Most movies (**not all**) are crap.

16

There's something likeable about French Canadians.

in Greece

17

The low class in Greece is really really low.

18

The older I get, the more I think that Leibnitz's expression "windowless monads" best describes what's going on.

19

Marcel Proust: terrible to read; important to know about.

20

Tourism is a joke: a joke on the tourists, a joke for the transporters, a joke for the servers, a joke for the arrangers, a joke for the explainers.

21

There's no getting around it: paper-thin prosciutto is heavenly.

22

I say again: I hope all mufflerless motorcyclists die a fiery death.

23

What makes people think they have the right (with their blaring radios, mounted loudspeakers, loud and raucous voices, streetside instruments, plastering machines, revving motors…) to inflict and spew forth their auditory excrement and garbage on any unsuspecting neighbor.

24

Music freaks (oh all and nothing but, the be-all end-all of one's existence!) invariably remind me of the "Big Ear" in Nietzsche's **Zarathustra**.

25

Nothing predisposes me more to accept the purist view of aesthetics than Greek music vis-à-vis the rest of things Greek.

26

I'm allowed at least one platitudinous entry:

The World is becoming homogenized.

27

Oh how many dainty and worldly and snobby and expert toes will be stepped on by this next entry:

(Except for a sense of timing), Greek food (at its best) is better than French food (at its best).

28

I never realized that Greeks can talk so beautifully...

about nothing.

(Astrology, for example.)

29

Greece after 46 years—still the land of the housefly.

30

I've never seen anyone dance like Fred Astaire.

The son-of-a-bitch just seems to walk on air!

31

Two things break me up every time without fail—with rolling tears and breaking voice:

When Monsieur Kazallon was thrown overboard and just opened his mouth to drown and die after so many horrors and privations. And then that wondrous line: "**Mon Dieu, l'eau est douce!**"

When the Peasant Marey comforted the little boy who thought he heard the cry "Wolf!", his big coarse thumb caked with loamy earth as he gently cradled the boy's face.

A kindness unknown to all except God.

back home

32

Eat only when famished, and sleep only when eyelids droop.

33

How **UNEVEN** human beings can be.

How adept, sensitive, able, virtuous in some things; and yet, the very same individual, how unaware, foolish, boorish, crass in others.

34

Sometimes I'm in the mood for the food in a greasy spoon.

35

An interest in genealogy shows a certain sensitivity/intelligence.

A surmounting of genealogy shows an even greater intelligence.

36

Somehow I've managed to survive,

In a world in which I do not participate.

37

I'm trying to decide who is more alien to me: Johnny Cash or Bill Frist.

Well, I guess Johnny Cash, for all of his darkness, hayseedness, and twistedness, was, at the least, still of this planet.

38

There are those who pursue patterns; and those who seek after the Existential Self.

Two very different things.

Many pattern-pursuers are psychological nincompoops.

39

I feel about Franklin Delano Roosevelt the way Esin feels about Mustafa Kemal Paşa.

40

Sometimes I think that **I'm** really the patriot.

41

There's something about food cooked right in front of you and immediately served…

That is most appealing.

42

I want to hear Ralph Nader apologize for costing Gore the election.

43

I don't think I would have liked the flower children and the whole Haight-Ashbury crowd.

In fact, I think I would have found them repulsive.

44

You can't beat an old beat-up car that still runs beautifully.

45

One of the most moving pronouncements in all of literature, Lord Glenarvan's final say to the soon-to-be-abandoned malefactor Ayrton:

> Now listen to my last words. You will be far removed from every land, and deprived of all communication with your fellow-men. Miracles are rare, and you will not probably remove from this island, where we leave you. You will be alone, under the eye of God, who reads the uttermost depths of all hearts; but you will not be lost, as was Captain Grant. However unworthy you may be of the remembrance of men, still they will remember you. I know where you are, and will never forget you.

46

So many doctors are so full of shit.

47

When it comes to felonies, misdemeanors, taxes, traffic… I obey all the rules.

I don't necessarily obey any other rules.

48

Why do I have to share this world with vulgarians, plebeians, peasants, thugs, rednecks, louts, coarse New Yorkers, loudmouths, clods, boors, bores, prissies, lap swimmers, football philosophers...?

49

I can hardly think of anyone more overrated than Sigmund Freud.

50

Dreams are closely related to indigestion.

51

There is something about **Writer's Digest** and all of its promotion-seeking, agent-searching, marketing-spinning, blog-making, book-signing, book-clubbing, book-touring, literary-festivaling, query-lettering, audience-pleading, advice-proffering camaraderie that just sickens me.

52

Globe Trekker reminds me of my own rough-and-tumble, winging-it, happy and uncomfortable travel days.

53

It just fascinates me: how much can be gleaned about a person from a few minutes of overheard conversation.

54

When I become The Dictator, I will commission a statue of Thomas Wolfe—**LARGER THAN ANY EXISTING STATUE ANYWHERE**—to be built right smack in the middle of that main square in Asheville, North Carolina.

55

Has Jules Verne ever written a book without a happy ending!?

56

I'm sure there are others somewhere out there very much like me; but I imagine finding them would be about as hard as winning the lottery.

57

I've been living on the edge, financially, for as long as I can remember.

I'm getting tired of it.

58

Not long ago, at the Hartsfield Airport in Atlanta, I sat by an English couple, all of us waiting to see what was to become of our delayed flights.

We exchanged a few pleasantries. A few short moments. And then lost in the shuffle of airport confusions.

And yet I'm convinced that these were two exceptional people, a chance and rare encounter, miraculously thrown my way.

I only wish I had gotten to know them better. Perhaps exchanged addresses. A wonderwork stroke of luck, now forever slipped away.

59

Professional travel writers, no matter how good they are: still whores.

60

The wonders of technology: so wasted on the clods to whom they have been bequeathed.

61

What hurts about the lottery: the clods who win it vs. the wondrous things **I** could do with it.

62

Mark Twain: whatever his strengths and virtues, **and there were many**, I can still do without the jokes and the twang.

63

The world is full of living cadavers.

64

A sudden dread disease still doesn't nullify the victim's previously earned repugnance and distaste.

65

Not long ago I learned that once Richard Pryor, while on a visit to Nairobi and watching the hustle-bustle of people going to and fro and about their business, remarked "There are no niggers here."

This caused a spurt of comprehension, a revelatory experience. (Akin to the first time I grasped the essential Darwinian idea.)

66

I love to watch Steven Seagal take on twenty thugs and adversaries at a time—karate chomps, breaking arms, snapping necks, gouging out eyes, walloping stomachs, kicking jaws...

But for Steven Seagal not a scratch. Not a goddamn teensy scratch!

67

There is something about the local news of Jacksonville (elections, committee meetings, proms, dinner theaters, the up and down headline exploits of the Jaguars, benefit galas, concerts, public hearings, quiltfests...) that just bores me to tears.

68

The car radio: the only time I can instantly shut up an asshole with the simple flick of my finger.

69

Isn't it interesting how I take to certain people even though I don't know much about their work, and am in no position to judge.

Example: Diego Rivera.

70

Certain writers (Robert Benchley, Andy Rooney, Stephen Potter, Max Beerbohm) deal with the **surface** of their experience.

The virtue of this: they **cannot** make a mistake.

71

Add Mitch McConnell to my Republican S-list.

72

There is some sense or other in which solipsism is inescapably true.

(And not, oh professional snots, not in any trivial tautological sense.)

73

It is that breathless **earnestness** of actors who do commercials that invariably induces vomit.

74

At Fork Union I carried the American Flag and declaimed "The Gettysburg Address."

I worship Thomas Wolfe, and have a high regard for Walt Whitman, John Dos Passos, Rex Stout, and Damon Runyon.

"Elmer's Tune," "Flat Foot Floogie," and "Chattanooga Choo Choo" are some of my favorite songs.

In spite of all my rantings and ravings, what could be more American than this.

75

Beyond sex, beyond fame, beyond fortune, beyond power, beyond vituperation, beyond cleverness, beyond "Truth"…

I wonder what's coming next. (Assuming, of course, halfway decent good health.)

Some things, however, never fade: family, friendship, wildflowers, **crème caramel**, cocktails, travel, literature…

76

Why anyone would use that vile-tasting, stinging, acrid, poisonous medicinal mouthwash (Listerine Peppermint, Scope Mint, Crest Antiseptic…all except Cinnamon Red) and swish it in his mouth is beyond me.

77

An able and dexterous short-order cook working in a busy and unrelenting Waffle House should be paid a **minimum** of $2,000 per week.

78

My God, I'm shrinking!

79

A cartoonist's few deft strokes, if they're the right strokes, speak volumes.

80

The **children** of celebrities don't very much interest me.

81

Karen Hughes: the quintessential androgyne.

82

This haunting thought keeps obtruding on my brain, and I don't know how to make sense of it:

"All times are simultaneous."

83

Convalescing is one of the premier and delightful experiences of humankind.

84

Romantic and limber and easygoing and charming as it is for things to be past schedule and late…

in the end I still prefer for things to be on time.

85

It's a shame that as people get older, they get hardened.

86

I've really known all along that goodness is the most important thing.

87

I wonder what it would be like to suspend all judgment.

88

There are good and bad people everywhere, I don't care if it's Yemen, Mongolia, Honduras, Namibia, Kazakhstan, or Uzbekistan.

And that goes as well for the North, South, East, and West of the United States of America.

89

I'm so glad and relieved that no one can read my mind.

90

Isn't it amazing that native speakers don't make errors of syntax, agreement, tense structure, etc. (Non-native speakers do.) After all, they **could** make such mistakes. But they invariably don't.

(Newton's apple **could** not have fallen to the ground. And it could even have gone up the other way.)

91

I've changed my mind about some things. And every so often I've changed my mind about changing my mind. And at times I've even changed my mind about changing my mind about changing my mind.

92

For years I lived in a Fool's Paradise, not really aware of all that was (**and is**) going on.

93

Pursuant to # **90**, isn't it also amazing that people don't make logical errors. That they blithely and invariably conform to the Principles of Contradiction and Identity.

94

I have an **ESPECIAL** animus for the Mafia.

95

In spite of all I've said and done, the truth is I'm really quite square.

96

Life/Death: this has now become the most imperious subject of contemplation.

All else is jabber and frivolity.

97

I'd like to borrow that Signature Phrase from NPR, even though it is hardly meant there as I would mean it. But I like it nonetheless:

All Things Considered

98

My head's about to burst!

Information Overload

Buffoons, One and All:

Entertainers, actors, Presidents, Presidential candidates, sporting idols, talk show hosts, revivalists, comedians, polemicists, news analysts...

100

95% of the "conversations" going on all around me are nothing less than **inane**.

101

I'm beginning to think overly-religious people are just plain retarded.

102

No matter how filthy rich I would get—even the Mega-Lottery should I win—I still would never have servants.

103

Time-travel is about as silly as voodoo and astrology.

104

The best Americans are those who bring a little bit of Europe to America.

105

One of my greatest pleasures recently is watching the History Channel's "Modern Marvels" and learning about how things work.

(And realizing how little I know about how things work.)

106

I wonder how many are aware of the wonder of a Wal-Mart Supercenter.

107

Whipped cream is **essential** to chocolate pudding.

108

A man suddenly gifted (by the aliens?) to speak every single language of the planet, including dialects and those of out-of-the-way tribal backwaters, **fluently and without a trace of accent**...

(Might be a good idea for a movie.)

109

The best chocolate is plain old chunky chocolate, without any admixture or attachment.

110

I have enormous respect for an able and honest auto mechanic.

111

Justice Antonin Scalia is an asshole.

This assessment is based not on evidence, reason, examination, deliberation...

No arguments, debates, discussions, dialectics...

Just diction, style, expression, body-language, smirks, rabidity, hubris...

(He reminds me of some of the philosophy snots at Cornell these ages ago.)

112

Mike Huckabee and Chuck Norris.

Birds of a feather.

113

I've always wanted to have a fondue where every single chunklet of meat was cut out of the very center of the center of a very finest filet mignon...

à la Farouk.

114

Jhumpa Lahiri: as good as J.D. Salinger.

115

I'm glad I did all my traveling during more innocent times.

116

Good musics: the music of the Andes; Greek music; Latin music; Caribbean music; East Indian music; Turkish music; African tribal music; Chinese classical music; Arabic music; old American music.

Bad musics: discordant American music; discordant jazz music; rap.

117

My God, all the things I've had to unlearn!

118

What ridicule, jokes, derisions, caricatures, lampooneries are heaped upon public figures.

Who in hell would want to be a public figure?!

119

It's very very hard to believe that T.S. Eliot wrote "Prufrock" at the age of 22.

120

"Voices are as distinctive as fingerprints."

Platitudinous as this may be, I only realized the truth of it relatively recently.

121

The English think they understand Greece.

What they understand is their own masquerade of Greece.

122

There's nothing at all better than a hot dog.

With mustard, onions, and relish.

At the right place, and at the right time.

123

I had no idea what old age, and all the problems of old age, was going to be like.

I must go back and compare notes with Logan Pearsall.

124

There is no more tasteless, revolting, and insulting culinary monstrosity than powdered eggs.

125

What a madhouse world it is, where everything is scripted.

126

I want nothing to do with any foodstuff that's "2%" or "Light" or "Fat Free."

127

I don't want to cook.

I want others to cook and prepare and serve and surprise.

128

I am not at all sure that the views of older men are more to be relied upon than those of younger men.

129

I love the thought of decent and courageous Italian prosecutors standing up to the Mafia.

130

Why do caps and gowns invariably make those graduating seniors look somewhat frowzy and unkempt?

131

The ugliest utterance in the English language: the word "dawwg" in a New York accent.

132

Oh how many novelists there are, and have been!

133

"Docudramas" are for the most part sickeningly **TERRIBLE**.

But an exception, reasonably well done and duly appreciated, was the one that had to do with the tragic 1977 crash of the two 747's on the tarmac at the Canary Islands.

134

What some old people may not realize is that they have been given the wondrous gift of being able to **REFLECT** upon so much that has happened to them without any compunction to **PERFORM**.

135

I really had no idea: amputees; paralytic stroke victims; victims of Parkinson's, cerebral palsy, Alzheimer's, brain tumors; aneurisms and embolisms; burn victims; victims of leukemia, lupus, rheumatoid arthritis; victims of lung cancer, pancreatic cancer, liver failure; detached retinas; asthmatics; depressives...

136

Oh how many poets there are, and have been!

137

No one **extrapolates** from a limited experience like a philosopher.

138

I have no desire, none whatever, to be: a soldier, a business man, an entertainer, an actor, an entrepreneur, a politician, a journalist, a Washington insider, a CEO, a dean, a cleric, a financier...

139

I wouldn't at all mind being: the dictator, a traveler, a gourmet, a sexual experimenter, an anthropologist, an archeologist, a linguist, an etymologist...

140

No matter how well-traveled, well-read, well-educated, widely experienced, long-living, long-suffering—one only gets a glimpse, a minikin glimpse, of the Whole.

141

General Douglas MacArthur: what a pompous, strutting, self-serving, theatrical ass.

142

I don't see why Hoyle's Steady State is necessarily incompatible with The Big Bang.

Why can't there be an endless series of expansions and contractions?

143

Trite perhaps, and certainly overworked, it is still the best and most poignant analogy for the human (and the cosmic) condition:

Like the sand castles at the seashore, lovingly and intricately carved, so finely sculptured...

In the end all to be utterly obliterated and washed away...

And as if they had never been.

144

Somehow, I've managed to survive and escape: out and in between a series of wars (too young, too old), hurricanes, earthquakes, tornadoes, volcanic eruptions, malaria and hepatitis and STD's and other horrific diseases, plagues and epidemics, air crashes (although a terribly close call), auto crashes (another terribly close call), (other close calls), fires, floods, sinkings, poisons, murderous confrontations, debilitating accidents...

And then there is Nona and Maya.

I haven't, though, managed to win the lottery.

But Lady Luck has not been unkind to me.

145

A terrible confession: I look forward to the next "Breaking News." And the direr, the better.

146

What is desperately needed: one able and benevolent and absolute planetary dictator.

147

I've always wanted to be **suffused** with happiness.

I wonder what it would take: a drug, a woman, a lotto ticket, a saint, a locale, a bo tree…?

148

The right place at the right time; the wrong place at the wrong time:

Two sides of the same coin.

149

One must **pay** for everything: food, water, clothing, haircuts, massages, doctors, nurses, therapists, lawyers, attendants…

I want to live in a world where payment is neither required nor expected.

(Like when we were children.)

150

There comes a point where the adverse opinions of literary and other critics just don't mean a damn.

151

Kirk Douglas playing Ned Land, Van Gogh, Spartacus…just makes me want to vomit.

(Especially Ned Land.)

152

I absolutely refuse to watch any fictional film based on the work of Jules Verne or Rex Stout.

153

Fireworks: color without meaning.

154

John Updike: I don't trust anybody who's so broadly endowed.

(A very high-class groupie, but a groupie nonetheless.)

155

Kazakhstan, Tajikistan, Azerbaijan, Uzbekistan, Turkmenistan... my geographical soul is just swamped and reeling!

156

Edward VIII's abdication speech to the British people: short, sweet, elegant, honorable, masterful.

157

The only time, so far, I've ever warmed up a bit to Winston Churchill: his approval of Edward VIII and Wallis Simpson.

158

I have contempt for academics, for they should be in charge, and they're not.

159

White House Press Secretary, State Department Spokesman, etc.: these have to be some of the slimiest, bootlicking, lackey jobs in the world.

160

Thomas Wolfe is a greater writer than: Sinclair Lewis, William Faulkner, John Steinbeck, Saul Bellow, and the black lady from Cornell.

(Not to mention Ernest Hemingway.)

161

I've made it abundantly clear that I detest, absolutely detest, motorcyclists without mufflers.

But I feel a certain gratitude and respect for motorcyclists with mufflers.

162

God isn't All-Powerful; He's just Omniscient.

163

Thomas Wolfe is on a par with Walt Whitman and Fyodor Dostoyevsky.

164

It doesn't matter that falling in love may not last; it is still one of the most precious and premier experiences of humankind.

165

I give a talk only **ONCE**; I don't give it a second time.

166

It has taken me 77 years to learn not to judge people too harshly.

167

I respect wolves; I loathe dogs.

168

What could be more unclassy than a tattoo.

(Especially on a female.)

169

It's hard for me to relate to any history that is pre-photography.

170

A supreme aesthetic experience cannot be planned ordered conjured scheduled…

It just happens.

171

Isn't it interesting that what was but a minor dalliance for Arthur Conan Doyle became, and rightly so, a dear and revered classic.

172

The mannerisms of teachers, professors, as they revel in their expertise:

A call for additional vomit.

173

Modern American music: country, western, country-western, jazz, blues, pop, hip hop, rock, hard rock, punk, rap…

A veritable wasteland.

174

It takes a lot of veggies to equal one slab of meat.

175

Some pre-photography writers who are still readable: Epicurus, Epictetus (Arrian), Rabelais, Montaigne, Jonathan Swift...

176

Shakespeare doesn't talk my language; I find him rather tedious.

177

Some of my sexual fantasies, you wouldn't believe!

178

Are giant cranes needed to make giant cranes?

And, if so, what about **those** cranes?

179

The **ONE** exception (**see #167**):

Old Barney (1993—2002) was a human disguised as a dog.

180

After I eat, I'm socially worthless.

181

I don't like people who don't like Jimmy Carter.

182

I've always wanted to find a restaurant where **EACH** fried oyster is cooked to order and placed piping hot on your plate, one after another, in luscious succession.

Ditto for tempura.

183

My father, from the Old World, was absolutely **incredulous** that tomatoes and potatoes came from the New World.

184

What sort of foul and filthy crud would throw out of a car window empty soda bottles, soiled cups and wrappers, whole cartons of trash, the accumulated butts of an ashtray—right onto a pavement and public thoroughfare.

Such vermin to be painlessly and instantaneously **zapped and eliminated** from the face of the earth.

185

The best pizza I've ever had:

Of all places, in Brussels, Belgium.

186

The part that luck plays in the affairs of men is enormous.

187

With microphones, there is no excuse whatever for speeches, harangues, and declamations.

188

Is this a bare possibility?

Aliens who are so **vastly** superior that they can, at their discretion, intervene in the affairs of men (and of this planet).

(Which makes prayer, just possibly, not as silly as it sounds?)

189

I sometimes wonder how anyone can come to have an overriding interest in anything other than food, drink, and sex.

190

Getting in touch with the Aliens may not be a matter of space probes, beamings, telescopes, S.E.T.I...

It may just have to do with **thinking the right thought**.

(Perhaps **They** have left a code for him who can decipher it.)

191

Although the Ontological Argument is in all probability a piece of verbal legerdemain, I have always been somewhat haunted by it.

192

Puppies and dogs are also (see # **58, 17th Encyclical**) two different orders of being.

(As are, vis-à-vis their elders, cubs, chicks, fawns, and baby hippos.)

193

I still have nightmares of Pinocchio being turned into a donkey, and of the cackling Wicked Witch in **Snow White**.

194

To give a speech that others have written: surely this must be the height of unselfrespect.

195

There's something about an **accident** that makes all those pretty theories seem ridiculous.

196

The Grand Caverns in Grottoes, Virginia, the small vegetable farms of Staten Island, the spacious outlying streets of Iraklion, the Jacksonville Zoo...

How simple, unpretentious, and delightful they were in the old days; what Monstrosities they have now become.

197

I haven't the slightest desire to jump out of an airplane in a parachute.

(Or be a NASCAR driver, march in a parade, collect celebrity autographs, and be a hotdog-eater champion.)

198

Some women are so good-looking on the outside but so messed up on the inside that even the primal desire to touch soon evaporates.

199

There are times when I'm a Christian in Greek; but definitely not ever in English.

200

I **LIKE** the old and original Thomas Common translation of **Zarathustra**—Professors Walter Kaufmann and Oscar Levy be damned.

(Anyone who would write an Introduction to a classic that is almost as long as the classic itself has to be a bona fide jerk.)

December 15, 2009

Ex Cathedra

19th Encyclical

von Herrn Doktor Professor Peter Joannides

1

Most of humankind:

Fragments interacting with fragments, nothing but fragments, even spouses, offspring, friends, colleagues…, fragments abutting brushing by fragments, all and everywhere fragments.

Only unto Himself is one a Wholeness.

2

I hate ads, any and all ads.

3

Driving through North Carolina, South Carolina, Georgia…listening to AM (and even FM) radio:

Amazing and hilarious, fatuous frothing entertainment.

4

A Joannidian haiku:

Waynesville (N.C.), late September morning, warm bright sunshine, 70°, people going to and fro, about their business, loaded pickups, traffic turns and lanes, banking, plumbers, roofers, fast food take-outs, shopping at Ingles.

5

I don't know which is worse, a redneck accent or a Brooklyn one.

(Since I was born and raised in and around New York City until the age of twelve, I can't help feeling a certain warmth for the latter.)

Let me put it this way: the redneck one is more alien, but the Brooklyn one is uglier.

6

There's no doubt about it: the History Channel's "Modern Marvels" is the best thing on television.

7

There are a lot of bimbos who vote in this world.

8

I like some people; and don't like others.

It's as simple as that.

(And no reasons tendered.)

9

It's fascinating: when I read **The New York Review of Books**, so many writers (artists, doers, personalities) I never even heard of; so many goings-on I had not the least inkling about.

10

There is such a thing as getting **beyond** Proust.

11

In my dining space, my sleeping space, my any place, **I don't want NO goddamn critters around**, either large or small.

12

The sound of an airplane: first from the movies, and **then** in real life.

13

Porno sex, virtual sex, machine sex, phone sex…ofttimes better than the real thing.

14

I know about economics even less than I do about physics.

15

Most people don't have the **time** to read.

16

John Updike: a vocabulary just a bit **too** good.

(Sort of like that of Patrick Leigh Fermor.)

17

John Updike: I had no idea about the psoriasis and the asthma.

This has taken me aback, and takes some of the sting out of my negatives.

18

I hate people who do their banking in a supermarket.

19

    It's hard to think of anything more disgusting than a Spanish bullfight.

20

    You can have the flamenco; I'll take the fado.

21

    Actors who don't do all that much for me: Marlon Brando, John Travolta, Mel Gibson, Sal Mineo (nothing at all), James Dean (nothing at all), Joan Crawford, Lauren Bacall, Chuck Norris, Harrison Ford, Henry Fonda, Kirk Douglas, Robert Taylor, Zsa Zsa Gabor, Clint Eastwood, June Allyson, George C. Scott, John Wayne…

22

Actors who do: James Cagney, Paul Muni, Humphrey Bogart, Fredric March, Robert Mitchum, James Stewart, Irene Dunne, Norma Shearer, Jean Arthur, Franchot Tone, George Sanders, Tyrone Power, Claude Rains, Louis Hayward, George Raft, Joseph Cotten, Ann Sothern, Claudette Colbert, Paul Henreid, Ida Lupino, Jack Carson, Spencer Tracy, Peter Sellers, Michael Caine, Olivia De Havilland, Deborah Kerr, Sydney Greenstreet, Gary Cooper, Walter Matthau, José Ferrer, Al Pacino, Cary Grant, Wallace Beery, Marlene Dietrich, Alec Guinness, Fred Astaire, Cornel Wilde, David Niven, Lee Marvin, Ronald Colman, Edward G. Robinson, Mickey Rooney, Fred MacMurray, Simon Signoret, Micheline Prelle, Doris Day, Peter Ustinov, Carmen Miranda…

23

Actresses who don't arouse me all that much: Marilyn Monroe, Rita Hayworth, Lana Turner, Esther Williams, Elizabeth Taylor, Ava Gardner, Betty Grable, Ursula Andress, Sophia Loren, Anita Ekberg, Jayne Mansfield…

24

Actresses who do: Paulette Goddard, Virginia Mayo, Joan Leslie, Barbara Rush, Laraine Day, Gloria De Haven, Susan Hayward, Linda Darnell, Hedy Lamarr, Ann Rutherford, Ruth Roman, Jean Peters, Joan Bennett, Arlene Dahl, Suzanne Pleshette, Eleanor Parker, Gina Lollobrigida, Silvana Mangano, Olga San Juan...

25

I actually fell in love with Barbara Rush and Laraine Day.

26

Comedians who don't do all that much for me: Milton Berle, Jerry Lewis, Will Rogers, Jim Carrey, Phil Silvers, Don Rickles, Lucille Ball & Desi Arnaz, Jerry Seinfeld & co., Chris Rock (nothing at all), Bill Cosby (absolutely nothing at all)...

27

Comedians who do: Sid Caesar, Richard Pryor, Laurel & Hardy, Jack Benny, Buster Keaton, Jack Oakie, Redd Foxx, Harpo Marx, Chico Marx, Lou Costello, Moe Larry & Shemp (**not Curly**), Benny Hill, Jackie Gleason, Billy De Wolfe, George Carlin, Janeane Garofalo, Buddy Hackett, Jonathan Winters, Bill Maher...

28

There's nothing like crisp and sunlit November days in Jacksonville, Florida.

29

I wish, just wish, that I would come home one day and somehow, suddenly, find **The Ibstick** just lying there on my desk.

30

What more sensible and all-inclusive philosophy of life: to be anti-pain and pro-pleasure.

31

John Updike has just written an article on Mars for the **National Geographic**.

An article on the career of Theodoros Kolokotronis and the Greek War of Independence is forthcoming, to be soon followed by one on the turmoil and contradictions in the inner life of the American poet Ben Belitt.

Another collection of poems and short stories is also in the offing, as well as a novel set in the interregnum period of colonial Malta.

32

I've always wanted to save this planet.

I don't say this humorously or flippantly, but in an earnest and heartfelt way. I've been mulling about it for a long time.

There are three possibilities that might come to pass, all of them **extremely remote**.

> 1. My work is published and disseminated, many see the truth and urgency of my political philosophy (Section XVI), and I am invested with dictatorial and unrescindable planetary power, afforded the utmost protection, and pursue my agenda.

(continued)

33

2.   I win the Mega-Lottery, and thus try to set in motion No. 1.

3.   I am visited and given awesome powers by vastly superior Aliens, who then leave it to me to take charge and begin to fulfill my vision. (Perhaps **They** will even stop my aging so I can complete my endeavors, or make it possible to transfer my powers to a successor.)

As I said, **EXTREMELY remote**.

34

I really had no idea of all the evil and ugliness in this world.

35

To need bodyguards wherever you go.

My God, what a way to live!

36

Even if it **is** David Niven playing Phileas Fogg—it is still sacrilege.

37

For me, graffiti is a breakdown of civilization.

38

When actors portray real people in real situations, it is a **BIG** turnoff.

And unwatchable.

39

There is no way to enjoy a cocktail standing up.

40

The Nobel Prize in Literature is **supposed** to be awarded to the best writer on the planet.

Oh to how many political ~~second~~ first-and-a-half-raters it has been bestowed!

41

I don't understand all this hullabaloo over cannibalism.

When necessary, protein is protein.

42

Oh so fondly do I remember all the many and varied clackety-clack clickety-click lickety-split hsssss shhhhh kuklung kuklung sounds of those bygone trains.

(See Wolfe, **Of Time And The River**, Sec. IV.)

43

So much of **modern** American music is simply an assault on the ear.

44

I have finally realized it, and have come to accept it: What I love most of all is **WORDS**.

45

After the advent of color photos, there really is no point to black-and-white ones.

No matter what all the artsy people say.

46

Is there an actor left who hasn't written an autobiography and shown us his baby pictures.

47

I like to think of God as a Witness.

A witness of what is true, **really true**.

48

There is something spiritually unclean about Joel Osteen.

49

What a beautiful and exhilarating thought:

Life is a certain surface scum found on certain minor planets.

50

My newly-emerging stubble of a beard: I begin to see and sense all sorts of dim atavisms rearing their hoary and prehistoric heads.

51

I don't mind some repetition in my **Ex Cathedras**.

52

Astronomers and astrophysicists nourish a special kind of hubris.

53

I never thought I'd find myself wondering if the current day will be my last.

54

I have been guilty, and still am, of road rage.

I'm working on controlling it.

55

I used to really like Jack Lemmon until he became such a philosopher of film.

56

COME THE REVOLUTION!

The following "sports" will be eliminated: football, boxing, rugby, car racing, skateboarding…

57

I'd like to know what sort of person writes those Instructional Manuals for electronic products.

58

I just don't understand economics.

The people are the same, the skills are the same, the tools and machineries are the same, the resources are the same...

Why is there a crisis?

59

Of all the literary genres—novel, short story, poem, play, essay— memoir/autobiography is the truest and the best.

60

For me, the ten greatest figures of literature and philosophy are (in very rough order): Logan Pearsall Smith, Friedrich Nietzsche, Jules Verne, Thomas Wolfe, Walt Whitman, Fyodor Dostoyevsky, H.G. Wells, Rex Stout, Robert Benchley, and John Dos Passos.

61

Honorable Mention: Francois Rabelais, Giovanni Boccaccio, Geoffrey Chaucer, Nikos Kazantzakis, Constantine Cavafy, Leslie Charteris, Arthur Conan Doyle, Edgar Allan Poe, Mark Twain, Franz Kafka, Ambrose Bierce, Aldous Huxley, Jack Kerouac, Marcel Proust, Emily Dickinson, Norman Mailer, T.S. Eliot, Arthur C. Clarke, Ayn Rand, Georges Simenon, Hermann Hesse, Damon Runyon, Mickey Spillane, George Orwell, Henry David Thoreau, Henry Miller, Homer Smith, Norman Douglas, James Hilton, Daniel Defoe, H. Rider Haggard, James Fenimore Cooper, Michel de Montaigne, Jonathan Swift, Max Beerbohm, Thomas Carlyle, Stefan Zweig, Ludwig Wittgenstein, Bishop George Berkeley, David Hume, J.D. Salinger, Bertrand Russell, Arthur Schopenhauer, Protagoras, Heraclitus, Democritus, Epicurus, Epictetus, Arthur Koestler, G.E. Moore, H.L. Mencken, Fred Hoyle, The Marquis de Sade, Eric Ambler, Graham Greene.

62

Addendum:

H.P. Lovecraft, Murray Leinster, Somerset Maugham, La Rochefoucauld, Plautus, Karl Kraus, Gore Vidal, Fredric Brown.

63

There are two traffic shit lights in Jacksonville, Florida: the one at Empire Point and Atlantic Boulevard, and the other at Ivey and Southside.

64

Of all the celebrities and entertainers, no one oozes and reeks of the worst sort of hubris more than Bill Cosby.

And yet I recently met a retired professor of the University of North Florida who makes Bill Cosby seem like a wide-eyed wingèd wondrous Angel.

65

My God, what if we're still not out of it when we die!

66

Why is it that a Southern accent repels me so—when I know many Southerners who are intelligent, sensitive, and decent?

67

There's nothing like watching C-SPAN:

When there's no talk; just pictures.

68

The "music" of Bruce Springsteen: just plain frenzied garbage.

69

I don't think I would have too many qualms about quickly and painlessly dispatching thugs.

70

"One evening along about seven o'clock I am sitting in Mindy's restaurant putting on the gefilte fish, which is a dish I am very fond of, when in come three parties from Brooklyn wearing caps as follows: Harry the Horse, Little Isadore and Spanish John."

This one line, **all by itself**, is enough to establish its author as a first-rate American writer.

71

God is nothing less than a Celestial Camera,

That records **EVERYTHING**.

72

Just about every painting—in all of its stillness, distortion, and self-consciousness—bores me.

73

I say again: There's a lot of crud in Jacksonville, Florida.

74

Has it ever occurred to you, perhaps only once in a long while, that the spectacle of people eating is downright disgusting?

75

There's no replacing: Joe Louis, Pope Pius XII, FDR, Johnny Weissmuller, Basil Rathbone, Joe DiMaggio, Sidney Toler, William Powell/Myrna Loy, Shemp.

76

Oh those documentary interrupters and fiscal solicitors—if only they knew how quickly they're zipped through.

77

Even from the grave, Updike contributes to **The New Yorker**.

78

The only paintings I've ever wanted to own:

"Daybreak" — Maxfield Parrish

"The Cossacks Jeering Reply to the Sultan" — Ilya Repin

"The Bargemen" — Ilya Repin

Landscapes — Diego Velásquez

79

When actors emote,

I decamp.

80

I miss those old drachmas.

81

I agree with Bill Maher.

"You don't fuck with an animal."

Especially a big one.

82

When does the President have time to think when he has so many functions to attend?

83

More repetition:

USA: the land of loonies.

84

There are times when I overhear a conversation at a neighboring restaurant table, or in the give and take of passers-by, or in the banter of the locker room at the gym—and the thought that comes to mind is this:

I have **ABSOLUTELY** no interest in any of your opinions about **ANYTHING** whatever.

85

Zadie Smith: Book Reviewer

I haven't read such amazing, high-flown, and pretentious gobbledygook since those Philosophy-of-Education Journals of years ago.

86

I love dirty talk.

87

When I'm really really starved and have a really really good steak, I know exactly how a hungry lion feels.

88

I've fallen in love so many times, I am dismembered.

89

Silvio Berlusconi commiserating with the victims of the recent earthquake.

Shit.

90

As long as there are wildflowers in this world, I've got to keep going.

91

All aspects merge in the Whole which is the Self.

92

I love rereading Simenon.

93

I spit on the Conquistadores.

94

Sometimes I get a glimpse of the limitations of my close friends, and it's a startling experience.

95

The Age of Letter-Writing is really over.

I don't know whether to rejoice or lament.

96

In the end, the music of the High Andes has to be given the top spot.

Even more so than that of Greece and of Latin-America.

97

Nothing could be more ridiculous than to have a prejudice, a dislike, for a whole people, a nation, a whole population.

Be that as it may, the closest to have earned such a ridiculous sentiment are, for me, the French.

98

I'm a bit proud of my contradictions.

99

Religion, for Greeks, is mostly a set of **practices**.

It has little to do with propositional beliefs.

100

See # **97**.

(Maybe also the Pashtuns and the Mexicans.)

101

I enjoy having a bit of nasty sex with men.

What I don't enjoy is the **smell** of a man.

102

Benjamin Netanyahu with his phony American accent.

103

For every one ept doctor, there are ten inept ones.

104

An ever and ever recurring sorrow and dismay: "I wonder whatever happened to …"

105

Flowers: living, breathing, exfoliating, pulsating…

They are not to be picked.

106

A nature documentary narrated by an English accent (for example, that of David Attenborough) **makes all the difference.**

107

Appetizers, Appetizers, bring 'em on Appetizers!

To hell with the main course.

108

I never again want to hear ice-water English during a Greek religious ceremony.

109

    It has recently occurred to me that my love of heavy rain and somber clouds—my profound and metaphysical sensibility—is easily transcended by an airplane climbing in a few minutes to an altitude in which skies are clear and the sun is shining.

This has devastated my profound and metaphysical sensibility.

110

Nostradamus is a joke.

111

    There are many whose intelligence is formidable and undeniable, but so circumscribed and flailing and delimited, that they might as well be considered stupid.

112

As a kid, I considered Sidney Toler the only true and authentic Charlie Chan.

As an adult, I decided that Warner Oland was the better Charlie Chan.

As a grand-adult, I have come back to Sidney Toler as the best Charlie Chan.

in Greece

113

George Seferis:

There's no way one can be a **great** writer and also an Ambassador.

114

Greek political commentators are about as inane as American ones.

115

Table-less and rustic roughing-it insect-ridden picnics are no longer for me.

116

In my old age, I am fiercely against **fiercely competitive** athletics.

I've managed to ruin both my shoulders and would gladly take my 95 glittering trophies and shove 'em all the way and the furthest up if I could just get my shoulders back.

117

Saul Bellow: **Humboldt's Gift**

What a pyrotechnic display of allusions and name-dropping and self-patting.

It outdoes Updike by about 10-1.

118

I must remember that all those literary gems with aching flaws were written by relatively young authors.

Just as my own work was.

119

I say again:

The two most beautiful languages in the world: Portuguese and Turkish.

120

My old high school buddy Nick Cassas went totally blind with detached retinas in both eyes more or less suddenly in his early-forties.

I think about him all the time.

121

What makes so many "important" writers somewhat adolescent is simply that they didn't live long enough.

Or, if they did, they no longer had the energy to keep writing.

122

Sometimes I'm just about to catch a **sub specie aeterni** moment. Perhaps a few minutes—perhaps only five minutes—later, but never **as it is happening**.

The thought of doing so is both frightening and exhilarating, and mystical.

123

It seems pretty obvious to me that what is desperately needed is a pyramidal planetary political Authority, with a benevolent, scientifically oriented, and absolute dictator at its apex.

124

Oh so many clever writers working **The New Yorker, The New York Review of Books, The Wall Street Journal,** the **International Herald Tribune, The Times Literary Supplement**...trying so so hard to be clever.

125

What's happening to me? Losing, slowly losing interest in so many things that I was so keen and passionate about not so very long ago.

126

"áma" and **"ótan"**

(This entry strictly for Greek speakers.)

Although I was brought up in a Greek household and spoke no English until the age of seven (and have been speaking a basic Greek ever since), I have never used the word "**ótan**." It was always "**áma**." Always. Even preceding the definite future tense.

(continued)

127

I don't know whether this is a Cypriot thing or an Asia Minor thing or an Ancient Greek thing or a Village thing or that I just wasn't paying attention to what people were saying—I honestly don't know.

But for me it was, and is, always "**áma**" and never "**ótan**."

128

People who throw a ball back and forth, forth and back to one another at the beach are idiots.

129

Oh if only I could be the dictator so that mufflerless motorcyclists could have six long jailhouse months to cool their heels.

130

PASOK and **Nea Dimocratia**

(Another entry more or less for Greeks.)

All my relatives and most of my friends in Greece seem to be on the side of **Nea Dimocratia**.

I can only register my contrary impression based certainly not on any real knowledge or experience but, as always, on (cultivated) immediate instinct and quick fancy and the seat of my pants.

(continued)

131

I seem to have a fairly positive regard for Mr. Papandreou, and as for Mr. Karamanlis the word that unfortunately comes to mind is "**fúscas**."

132

See # **119**

Japanese spoken and sung by breathless young girls is right up there with them.

133

For all the knocks and aspersions I've made about both of them over the years, in hindsight what better and more benign places to be from and go to than Jacksonville and Rhodos.

134

Those who have "been everywhere" and "seen and done everything" because they were in the service or the merchant marine—have always amused me.

135

The more time goes by, the more I like Aliki Vouyouklaki, despite all the sweet sugary sentimental reasons not to.

136

Every so often a wave of remorse: so so sorry for so many things I did; and for so many things I didn't do.

137

A Little Note For My Biographers

The spelling of "pyjamas" with a "y" was **not** an affectation. It had to do with all those English writers I was exposed to in school.

When I realized that in America it's spelled with an "a," it was much later, and I really saw no good reason to change it.

138

Wittgenstein again?

How come I speak English and not Moldovan? How come I was born into this family, this era, this milieu, and not into one in Africa or China or Sumatra? What is this **I** that seems to hover and transcend all the accidents of time and place and circumstance?

139

NO MORE soldiers, soldiering, shooting, slaughtering, carnage.

140

Two sorts of people intimidate me:

1. Those who speak many languages (**well**).

2. Gourmets.

141

I like just about all the musics of this world, except for **modern** American shrieking-mumbo-jangle.

back home

142

Celebrity actors who do ads make me sick.

143

After all these years, to suddenly realize that Don Knotts was quite a likeable character.

144

Except for the aches and pains, old age is really as wondrous as early age.

(Layers and layers of persuasons, prejudices, idées fixes, assumptions, presuppositions, compulsions, certainties, loyalties, monomanias…come sloughing, one after another, come sloughing sloughing off.)

(I am somehow reminded of **The Incredible Shrinking Man**, especially its ending.)

145

Obama's speeches are much too long.

146

If I were the planetary dictator, it would then be:

No one above the law, except me.

147

John King and his maps:

The Human Computer

148

If you don't write it down, forget it.

149

I'm no overwhelming fan of Robert Frost, but I do like that one line:

"I only go / When I'm the show."

150

If I had the energy, I would write about all the chimeras and eidolons that have entrapped and dallied with my mind over the years.

151

Golf isn't really such a bad game, except for the business types who play it.

152

What monumental absurdity, stupidity, tragedy: soldiers, on both sides, obeying their asinine generals.

153

A reminder to all the rabid partisans and zealots: little children are the same all over the world.

154

A very close friend of mine absolutely detests Dan Rather of CBS; another dear friend absolutely can't stand the sight of Senator Patrick Leahy of Vermont.

I just don't understand it.

(But maybe they wouldn't equally understand my absolutely virulent distaste for Senator Phil Gramm of Texas.)

155

If I had been living in the 19th Century, I probably would have taken extra good care of my horse.

156

For all we know, Eugene V. Debs may have been a better man than all the revered idols of the American pantheon of political luminaries.

157

I love to visit very remote and hardly known islands.

158

Some natives eat insect grubs with as much gusto as I do fried oysters.

159

Science, with an American accent, just doesn't cut it.

(Science, with an American accent, forfeits all of its splendour.)

160

The real truth is, were I to really become the absolute planetary dictator, I would probably delegate all those awesome responsibilities to those whom I deemed to be capable, honorable, and effective (probably, mostly Scandinavians), and then sit back, oversee, and enjoy life.

161

My God, how **topical** all of our pronouncements and enthusiasms will seem 100 years from now.

(Sort of like elaborate critiques of silent film stars that nobody remembers.)

162

All my life I've been casting pearls before the wrong audience.

163

Actors portraying, mouthing real people.

This has to be the height of dramatic rubbish.

164

The Holidays, in order of importance:

    New Year's Eve
    Christmas
    Halloween
    Thanksgiving
    Labor Day
    Memorial Day
    Valentine's Day

    (continued)

165

    Easter
    Mother's Day
    Father's Day
    Lincoln's Birthday
    Martin Luther King Day
    Columbus Day
    Washington's Birthday
    The 4th of July

166

If I were wealthy, I'd be a more-than-generous tipper.

167

It's too bad that **Planet Earth** was not narrated by a male.

168

Dessert should be had **with** the main meal, for the delightful contrast.

169

To those who would urge me to try to publish parts of my work, I say:

I am not a fragment.

In any case, the "parts" are too interconnected.

170

Obviously, I'm a sucker for a British accent.

171

From the maw of the lottery won, all sorts of things would erupt and flow forth.

172

Bird watchers, animal lovers, dog enthusiasts, those in Yellowstone who dutifully maintain their place in a traffic line so that they can catch a glimpse of the grizzlies—binoculars and cameras and "ooh"s and "ahh"s to the ready…

There's something a bit off about these people.

173

My God, we've got to ask Fowler! Fowler is the impeccable master. Fowler will give us the definitive answer. Fowler is The Great Authority.

174

The Elements of Style is really a WASPy little book.

175

I wonder why vegetarians don't consider what they do to plants also a form of murder.

176

Dow Jones, Standard & Poor's, Nasdaq, Index of Leading Economic Indicators, Capital Gains, GDP, IRA, Hedge Funds, Mutual Funds, Mortgage-Backed Securities, Subprimes...

you might as well be talkin' Chinese.

177

I wonder if one day white people will be looked upon as some sort of curious albinos.

178

The Spanish radio station in Jacksonville reminds me wistfully of long-ago Prodromidis in New York.

179

What makes concert-goers think there is anything particularly interesting in watching the **making** of music (with fingers strumming, shoulders up-and-down saw saw-sawing, mouths blowing, pursing, poomp poomp-poomping, etc.).

180

The emptier the stomach, the greater the alcoholic epiphany.

181

As an Introducer to the ways and wonts of a foreign land, I'll take the **Globe Trekker** gals over Christiane Amanpour anytime.

182

I could tell that South Koreans were hustlers ever since 1960 when I first set foot in Seoul.

183

There is nothing quite so off-putting as American accents slumming and traipsing around Third World countries.

184

Ken Burns: Magnificent as some of his documentaries are, there's still that touch of sentimentality.

185

Football is a brutal game, and should be outlawed.

186

Men unshaven for a few days may be squeaky clean, but they still look dirty.

187

If I were to hit the lottery, it would be mostly travel and food, and not much else.

188

A Book Review by Prof. John R. Searle in **The New York Review of Books**, September 24, 2009:

A prime example of Philosophical Horseshit.

189

      Tugging at me, tugging tugging, all sorts of chimeras, memories, wisps, griffins, early childhood wraiths, Proustian wonderments, Manhattan lights and blinkings screams, subway smells and the squeal of the South Ferry local, the railing on the Staten Island ferry, old girlfriends and undying loves, handball triumphs and defeats, revered books, a confusing jumble of times, the wandering Maryland years, the Virginia years, the Jacksonville years, the pilgrimages to Greece, the sexual obsessions, **sub specie aeterni** moments, Maya a baby, Maya now, Nona then, Nona now, old professors, the South American rain forest and alpacas on the high plateau, colleagues and friends, and colleagues and friends dying off, moments of cowardice embarrassment insensitivity, the neighborhood kids in Lodi shooting pellets and lighting punks in the nearby brambly field, the Fork Union drills and uniforms, the depressions elations angers wishful thinkings, illnesses and operations fears, accidents, a thousand expansions of this list, a moment of perfect weather and the fall of leaves, a frozen winter morning in Germany and snow-bound branches, the Bendix Diner and bicycle jaunts up and down the daunting hill, like a reel an ever changing kaleidoscopic reel, a back-and-forth reel, all mixed and re-mixed, reversed re-reversed…

      like the whirlwind that Marlon Brando once mentioned, the whirlwind roaring and embrangling and not to be made sense of.

190

I think quite a few Republicans are just plain creeps.

191

Pain is an absolute.

And that includes the pain of animals.

192

Hendrik Hertzberg: whatever else may be said about him, he's a damn good writer.

193

TV's **Modern Marvels**

All those engineers, scientists, truck drivers, mechanics, historians, experts, factory hands…make me feel like a literary popinjay who knows next-to-nothing about so many things, and who is just beginning to realize the complexities and intricacies of how things work.

194

One thing you can safely say about me:

He never let fame go to his head, for there was never any to go.

195

William Safire

I didn't have much use for his politics, but I respected his knowledge and love of language.

196

You **do** usually get what you pay for.

197

To repeat and super-add: I would have no qualms whatever in vaporizing tattooed thugs.

198

If there's one thing I can't stand, it's a salad with egg in it.

199

How I admire those who can wrestle with alligators, pythons, steers...

As for me, I'm deathly afraid of all large, and even moderately large, animals, including horses, dogs, cats, cows, and parrots.

I can probably handle little chicks and baby rabbits.

200

Everything that happened had to happen exactly as it did happen and couldn't have happened any other way.

"What might have been is an abstraction

Remaining a perpetual possibility

Only in a world of speculation."

December 15, 2010

Ex Cathedra

20th Encyclical

von Herrn Doktor Professor Peter Joannides

1

Alcohol opens up the sluices of the mind.

To those who would denigrate it, I say: "You don't know what the hell you're missin'."

2

The **CLEAN LINE** encloses and perimeters:

Norway, Sweden, Finland, Iceland, Denmark, Holland, Germany, Switzerland, Austria, Bolzano, Slovenia(?), the Baltic States(?), Singapore(?).

Whatever lies on the other side of this line is not so clean.

3

If it weren't for the legal constraints and consequences, I think I could probably shoot to kill someone who deliberately throws a piece of chewed gum onto a public pavement.

4

Whenever I see a Republican senator from the Deep South, I can't help what happens:

The phrase just seems to suddenly and involuntarily leap to my lips: Southern Shit.

5

If ever there's a woman who is "my type," as they say, it has to be Daljit Dhaliwal.

6

When a writer gets famous, corruption invariably sets in.

(It's a shame that as good and perceptive and sensitive a writer as Jhumpa Lahiri is, she has now to exemplify this.)

7

    Only in America are the sorriest tomatoes actually served at a dinner table.

8

    Please don't ask me to take part in all your collective lunacies and sentimentalisms.

9

When travelling: a huge breakfast, a light lunch, a good dinner.

    When stationary: a light breakfast, a huge (apéritif) lunch (siesta), a moderate dinner.

10

    Add Daljit Dhaliwal to my harem.

11

There are more philosophers at the "Y" than you can shake a stick at.

12

Those early childhood experiences, those of glee and wonder, transcend and overstep and put the lie to all the tragedies, depressions, desolations, blows and afflictions that may soon follow.

13

I love and admire a good heist.

14

When you come right down to it, the whole concept of God is pretty much meaningless.

Not false, just without any clear meaning.

15

Syrian and Palestinian Arabs: probably the most genuinely hospitable people in the world.

16

Those acts of help and succor, those of goodness and kindness, transcend and overstep and put the lie to all the tragedies, depressions, desolations, blows and afflictions that may soon follow.

17

Technology

We're all caught up in it; nobody really understands it; it is irreversible and cannot be undone; it probably couldn't be duplicated starting from scratch; it may be using us, and not us it; …

It has a life of its own.

18

How many quiet forgers have tipped the balance of history, averted dire catastrophes, started transformational changes, perhaps saved thousands and thousands of lives…

and are wholly unknown.

19

Oh how many Heads of State had their moment of glory.

Only to be unceremoniously cut down a few short years later.

20

The Big Four: Logan Pearsall Smith, Friedrich Nietzsche, Jules Verne, Thomas Wolfe.

After that, no matter what, there's a little bit of a drop.

21

Who cares what Isaiah Berlin thought.

About anything or anyone.

22

I don't trust anybody who's not a determinist.

Who would try to wriggle out of something so palpably true.

23

Eulogies are usually sickening.

And, in considerable measure, sickeningly untrue.

24

A white Florida bird, a sort of small egret, graceful and dainty, with its long thin legs somehow trying to dodge and make it in the midst of Jacksonville bustle and traffic.

What more wistful and poignant.

25

Only a self-propelled writer (artist) is truly free.

All others are just employees.

26

George Will is a little bit of a smart-ass.

27

Spare me, please, from **Masterpiece Theatre**.

28

What with all the pirouettes, theatrics, garbages that the President has to go through, is it any wonder that no self-respecting person would want to be President.

29

NPR

Although I know not the bodies and the faces, there are the **Voices**.

Which have a Reality of their own.

Carl Kasell: warm and avuncular whom I have been listening to for more years than I care to remember. Like family. The Walter Cronkite, or shall I say the Frank Blair, of Radio.

Steve Inskeep: a little too upbeat and enthusiastic for my taste. And a bit patronizing.

(continued)

30

Robert Siegel: a kind of intellectual know-it-all, but pleasant enough.

Linda Werthheimer: pleasant enough.

Michele Norris: pleasant enough.

Neal Conan: a grating voice. I have to switch off or change the station. More or less what happens when O'Reilly appears on television.

Richard Gonzales: pleasant enough.

Scott Simon: pleasant enough.

Mara Liasson: the hard voice.

Allan Cheuse: oh so many literary masterpieces, lying around all over the place, one after another.

Andrei Codrescu: one should be clever and witty, by all means.

Diane Rehm: hang in there, Diane.

(continued)

31

    Silvia Poggioli: definitely good and my type of person and likeable—would love to visit all the haunts of Rome with her.

    Linda Gradstein: a Stateside Jewish girl, immersed in her Jewishness, but trying to be fair and balanced.

    Nina Totenberg: pleasant enough.

    Ann Taylor: is this a human being or a disembodied computerized Voice-Machine?

    Susan Stamberg: another Jewish lady, immersed in her Jewishness.

    Terry Gross: there are other subjects besides modern American jangly music.

    Bob Mondello: sounds like a fag to me.

    My favorites:
    Brian Naylor
    Corey Flintoff

32

Somehow, I'm supposed to like jazz.

All my friends, all the critics and intellectuals, the American and even European cognoscenti, say so.

I'm sorry; it just doesn't do anything for me.

33

I think I may have once met Arthur Koestler.

It must have been sometime in the early- or mid-sixties when I was with Maryland, somewhere in Europe, probably Germany.

I was sitting in a hotel restaurant and he was at a table across the way, watching me in an amused and attentive way, and finally motioning to me to join him. I went to his table, or he came to mine, I don't remember.

(continued)

34

We chatted for about 30 minutes or so, about some heavy subjects. (I think Wittgenstein was mentioned.) He told me his name was "Zimny," or something like this. Apparently we were staying at the same hotel, because I became somewhat intrigued by him and later knocked on his door, but there was no response.

Of course, I'm not at all sure it was Koestler, but in retrospect he certainly looked very much like some of the photographs I've seen of the renowned author. I have a feeling it was, but, as I said, not at all sure.

It was an utterly chance encounter.

35

The commendable thing about Burt Wolf's globe-trekking is that he emphasizes one of the most important aspects of good travel: **FOOD**.

36

"…for our children and our grandchildren"

I think if I hear this phrase one more time, I'll start screaming.

37

I take second place to nobody.

38

There are really no conspiracies. (Except in the literal sense that there are conspiracies.)

There are only lost souls, from the lowliest to the highest.

In that Wolfian sense of "lost."

Wolfe himself probably had not much idea of the **philosophical** import of his idea of "lost."

But no one has ever said it more beautifully.

39

Ian Wright

The travel program is not about **YOU**, asshole; it is about the country you're visiting.

40

There are well-behaved little children; and then there are little shits.

My God, what a difference!

41

I still like Obama (and quite a bit); despite the obvious vanity.

42

I have finally realized that Greek conversationalists, clerics, politicians, television personalities, and the like, aren't so profound, superior, quick, insightful; they just have a greater facility with the language.

43

Americans are generally disposed and coached to take orders.

If only we had someone to give the right orders.

44

I keep defending judgments made on the basis of (cultivated) gut-feeling and (cultivated) instinct.

I don't think I have been too often wrong in my assessments.

A case in point: the philosopher John Rawls.

I remember taking a course in Ethics with him at Cornell. I hardly remember what was said so long ago. (I do distinctly remember his struggle with speech.) I have read practically nothing of his work.

And yet I will attest that here was a man of integrity, moral courage, and probably rigorous and enlightened thinking. A good man in every way.

45

An imaginatively laid-out liquor store with its array of bottles of all sizes and shapes and sparkling colors, and all the potential wonders locked within, is one of the most beautiful things on earth.

46

What's going on? **What the hell am I doing here?** What have I to say to anyone who likes Country Music!

47

"O lost, and by the wind grieved, ghost, come back again."

What is it about this line that has obsessed my mind for over 60 years!

All I have to do is have a couple of drinks and it unveils itself and gushes forth from my lips.

48

Prime Minister's Questions: British House of Commons

What a rollicking punctilious minuet!

49

There's something about potholes that makes me curse roundly those responsible.

50

In some of the old crime and adventure movies, whenever there was a scene in which a briefcase would be flipped open to reveal a chock-full of stacks and stacks of $100 bills,

I would swoon with pleasure, envy, and delight.

51

Once upon a time, in my travels, I had a choice—either explore the delta of the Danube or visit Braila.

I chose Braila.

It was one of the stupidest choices I ever made.

52

So many doctors are scumbags.

53

Add Senator Jeff Sessions to my Republican S-list.

54

Archie Goodwin

I love the way Archie talks, describes, reacts, acts, surmises, quips…

He's just about my favorite character.

55

The best-prepared fried shrimp are definitely kin to the best-prepared **loukoumáthes**.

56

I never thought I'd ever hear myself saying this!

"Sex is finally becoming a bore."

57

Oh how many emulators, mimickers, practically look-alikes.

But, in fact, nothing less than the "grunting pig"s of Zarathustra.

58

Modern-Day Cruises

What adventure!
What explorations of foreign lands!
What startling memories and unexpected insights!

59

I have an interest in just about anything Bill Maher has to say.

60

I've always wanted to periodically get together with a small group of intelligent and personable friends to discuss various and sundry matters.

Over the years, I've managed at times to achieve this, but certainly not as often as I would have liked.

61

I'm too old to be corrupted.

62

The only way to truly enjoy a drink is to be reclined, preferably alone, and **not to have to move**.

63

I have an interest in just about anything Gore Vidal has to say.

64

Lectures and Lecturers:

So so passé.

65

Campbell Brown

She grows on you.

66

There are more diagnosticians, nutritionists, physiologists at the "Y" than you can shake a stick at.

67

Every time I don't win the lottery, I think of Kazantzakis' Priest Fotis picking up the pieces and resuming the interminable march toward the east.

68

Two of my pet dislikes: Luna Parks and Game Shows.

69

All those attractive female newscasters:

In my mind's eye, I undress them all—stark naked do I review them.

70

With enough money, just about anything can be done.

71

Whenever I've had a violent argument with someone, 80% of the time I was in the right; 20% in the wrong.

72

Mark Levin: a real nutcase.

73

If I had to do it over again, I would:

Not spurn the advances of certain gay men.

Play racquetball with and teach Nona when she asked me to.

Not have that terrible argument with Mama in Venice about gifts and souvenirs.

Explore the delta of the Danube instead of visiting Braila.

(continued)

74

Not break down and cry in front of Mason G. Daly when I was about to be fired from my Maryland job.

Never ever fly a little airplane.

Really look carefully, and extra carefully, when pulling out into traffic.

Not play handball so ferociously that my health was compromised.

Give up the second game after winning the first and go for the 11-point tiebreaker.

(continued)

75

Not have all those grain drinks for so many years instead of wine.

Follow my mother's advice that one should get up from the table a little bit hungry.

Try to muster more courage and fearlessness.

Not have spent so much time chasing after girls rather than exploring the sights.

Have learned at least Spanish and French (and maybe Italian).

(continued)

76

    Have given more time and attention to the Aesthetic dimension of things.

    Have made every effort to have three more children.

    Have found some way, no matter how difficult, to have my work published, and on my terms.

    Have spent more time in the Far East instead of Europe.

    Have learned a bit more about finance and economics.

(continued)

77

Have appreciated a certain Japanese girlfriend more than I did.

Have spent more time with my father.

Have gone to see the boy when he came to Disney World.

(continued)

78

Have checked into a first-tier hotel in crisp and delightful Ambato that first day after spending almost two weeks in the Ecuadorean jungle with the Canadian entomologists—sweaty, filthy, wash-less, and on an all-night bus—instead of a second-tier hotel, and forever forfeiting that first wondrous shower in a more ambient setting. (And checking into the first-tier hotel the next day anyway, and spending a week there. **Forever concerned about the goddamn money.**)

Have been more flexible when travelling with all my toiletries, handball gear, swimming gear, books and magazines, overpacking, etc.

The list could be longer.

79

Robert Culp, Bill Cosby: **I Spy**

Here we have two actors, one without any hubris (he may have had other faults, but not an ounce of hubris); the other with hubris coming out of his ears.

80

Bill O'Reilly: the closest thing yet to a real Devil.

81

The idea that Faulkner was a greater writer than Wolfe makes for gales and gales of laughter.

82

I feel this terrible guilt and responsibility toward those who have labored for years and years at boring, hazardous, numbing, and repetitious jobs to in some way, however slight, contribute to their deliverance.

83

What chance do little children have with some of the parents they were given.

84

Whenever I see someone walking his or her large dogs—tugging and pulling on their leashes—

I feel a certain immediate revulsion and disgust.

85

"Why do soldiers obey orders?"

This should be the subject of intense scrutiny.

With the objective of realizing its negation.

86

What chance do parents have with some of the parents **they** were given.

87

Just about anything, no matter how pure and unblemished and sacrosanct, can be Hollywoodized.

88

Viennese intellectuals around the turn of the century:

Quite a group.

89

All the spoofs and ridicule to the contrary, that's exactly the way it is:

The Ghost in the Machine.

90

I have measured out my life with lotto tickets.

91

Heisenberg with his Indeterminacy Principle is a sophistical asshole.

Just because we cannot **know** how something is doesn't mean that how something is, is not determined.

92

I need to be discovered.

93

I don't particularly like Chief Justice John Roberts.

94

Newt Gingrich

Almost all the time, I haven't the foggiest what he's talking about.

95

The worst thing about Jimmy Carter, whom I very much like and respect, is that he likes the music of Willie Nelson.

96

There is something about ginger that is mystical.

97

All these years, these years after years, I thought Monsieur Kazallon was a Frenchman. Now I have suddenly come to realize he was an Englishman from London.

HOW COULD I HAVE MADE SUCH AN ERROR!

98

Recreational Dune Buggies: the ugliest, noisiest, most disgusting, grotesque, obscene of all modern contraptions.

99

    Some ordinary Bar&Grill in some nondescript strip mall in some workaday neighborhood in some commonplace suburb in some middling metropolis—

    may have some of the most amazing food imaginable.

100

    Writers, literary critics, book reviewers, commentators who write as if there were a common fund of knowledge that any half-educated reader would and should be privy to—with all their allusions, eruditions, name-droppings, French phrases, etc. —make me sick.

    I can spot such phony cockadoodledoos within three or four paragraphs.

    (I am always in a fog, and learn new things every day—things that many already know.)

101

    There's something ridiculous about talking about nations as if they were people.

102

On an empty stomach:

I don't want to read, write, have sex, socialize, think.

On a really empty stomach:

All I can think of is having a drink—(and then **maybe** socializing).

103

I'd like to think that Wolfe wouldn't have done an Alpo ad even for 100,000 (1936) dollars.

104

I've finally figured out what it is that's wrong with Ayn Rand:

She's unidimensional.

105

Huxley wanted to go out in a blaze of glory—with loads and loads of LSD.

I want to go out in a blaze of haute cuisinery—with loads and loads of triple-cream brie.

106

It's a sin to be in Jacksonville in June, July, and August.

107

When I win the lottery, I'm going to hire Burt Wolf to take me to all those high and low restaurants, world-wide, and order for me, and explain and enlighten.

108

It seems to me that communism, in its essence, is quite correct.

109

Cialis Ads

Those actors' knowing looks, the winked complicities, the sly and sheepish immodesties—

not only makes me want to vomit, but double-vomit.

110

There is roughly one dwarf for every 40,000 births.

This means that in Jacksonville with a population of over a million there should be, statistically speaking, about 25 dwarfs.

I think I have only once caught a glimpse of one in all the years I have been here.

And yet I know they must exist.

And that they wonder, and make the best of their lot.

111

Spare me, if you please, from any official duties, speeches, positions, adulations, responsibilities, answerabilities.

112

I no sooner pick up the Sports Page, than I put it down.

113

The children of my friends aren't the same as my friends.

114

Great men are considerably more than the measure of their commentators.

115

The most magnificent building in the United States of America:

The Library of Congress, Washington, D.C.

116

By rights, sex is and should be, tied to all the higher echelons of life.

117

Pretty much, just a minute or two of hearing or watching anything, and I know what it's all about.

118

I have nothing to say to tattooed men.

As for tattooed women, I run the other way.

119

I am constantly being eviscerated by this or that, but in the end I come back to Myself.

120

It's hard enough to know what goes on inside a human, much less an animal.

121

Sometimes I think about all those I have skewered, and that they have family, and have children, and are fathers and mothers…
        and wish I didn't have to skewer them in that capacity.

122

I'm sick and tired of hearing what 25-yr-old Alexis de Tocqueville had to say about America 175 years ago.

123

Just think of it, in all these endless immensities of space, a watery planet!

124

I've always been fascinated by **real** time-lapse fast-forward photography.

125

To enjoy sex, one has to be in sexual mode.

126

I don't like ads, and I don't like people who do ads.

127

Sometimes I think I could eat raspberries all day long.

128

75% (and maybe more) of handicap-sticker users are frauds.

(Including myself.)

129

What makes actors (and former network anchors) think that anyone is interested in their philosophical opinions.

130

Myself: the Spider in the middle of its web.

131

If I had had the time and energy, I would like to have written a little essay entitled:

"What is there to like about a large dog?"

132

If only the CNN newscaster Susanne Malveaux didn't have such a terribly American accent.

(The same could be said for the actress Catherine Zeta-Jones and the Weather Girl Bonnie Schneider, except that with Bonnie the accent is more or less fitting, and besides, the overwhelming sex appeal overwhelms the objection.)

133

One of these days, I'm going to do a piece on "Swimming Pool Etiquette."

(And the lack thereof.)

134

It isn't politicos, CEO's, gangsters, Popes and Archbishops... that are diabolical.

The truly diabolical are English professors.

135

I've never really met anyone like myself, but I suspect there are others—

scattered few and far between.

136

In my old age, thanks to print but more so to television, I feel a bit like Buddha when he left his sanctuary.

137

A thought worth repeating:

Modern American music is mostly garbage.

138

I have quite a lot of respect for engineers.

139

American culture: the word that quickly comes to mind: impoverished.

140

I insist: You cannot read a part of my work without reading the whole of my work.

141

It's either too fucking hot, or it's too fucking cold.

142

The one impression I have of Henry Miller, given the minuscule time I spent with him, is that he would smile only when something was really worth smiling about, and laugh only when something was truly risible and funny.

143

Some of my best friends are French.

(Just as they could easily be Pashtun or Mexican.)

144

Right after I eat, I want to lie down: No delay, no putting things in their place, no worry about refrigerated items, no chitchat...

145

There's something about teachers—just about **ALL** teachers—that is sickening and repellent.

(Except, of course, for Professors Gordon and Lehman—University of Virginia—1948-1951.)

146

I'm all for Tex Beneke and "Kalamazoo" and "Chattanooga Choo Choo."

147

If only we could relive those early times in all their intensity and immediacy,

    and still be us.

148

I wonder if people and critics realize that "The Gods Must Be Crazy" was a superb film.

149

"Nothing that makes us happy is an illusion."

Coming from Goethe, that's something to think about.

150

I despise those who don't do their job well.

151

I don't want my red wine at room temperature.

I want it a teeny bit chilled.

152

Maya's famed Gringlish line:

"One C-SPAN **ftáni**."

153

The so-called "Common Man"

More often than not, what an ugly creature.

154

I don't want my wine **with** my meal. I want it **before** my meal.

Sort of like a cocktail.

155

Tony Judt: What a terrible and heart-rending personal tragedy; but what a show-off as a writer.

156

Sometimes the Weather Channel on TV is the only thing worth watching.

If only for the soft music.

157

I wonder if women who wear earrings realize that one day this may be regarded as not too far removed from the practice of the Ubangi who distend their lips.

158

The quintessence of sleaze: Dick Morris.

159

Jules Verne

Claudius Bombarnac, Special Correspondent may not be as popular or well-known as some of the Master's other works, but it ranks right up there with the best of them.

The same can be said for **The Tribulations of a Chinaman**.

160

The older I get, the more I realize that the philosopher Norman Malcolm was a prime-grade creep.

161

There's something frightening about being a vegetarian.

162

Sometimes I think I could eat brie all day long.

163

Those old ladies with frizzled white hair and saggy wizened skins were once comely young girls.

164

Ex Cathedra 18, # 160

To those who may be wondering why Isaac Bashevis Singer was left off the list, it's because he may very well have deserved the Award.

165

Ex Cathedra 19, # 27

I forgot to add Mel Brooks to the list of comedians who do all that much for me.

166

It's uncanny: Gwen Ifill reminds me of my cousin Doris up in New Jersey.

167

No matter how agnostic, atheistic, liberal, uninvolved a Greek may be, he still would never **dream** of not baptizing his children.

168

Sarah Palin: ambitious and dangerous.

169

Ex Cathedra 19, # 56

I forgot to add bungee jumping and skydiving to the list of idiocies.

170

Pope Benedict XVI: oh how he just **loves** being the Pope.

171

Max Beerbohm is a much more important writer than most everyone realizes.

172

How I regret not partaking of all the culinary marvels scattered here and there and in all the many niches of this planet.

173

I've never sent a stamped self-addressed envelope to anybody.

If there's so little simple courtesy left in the world, then fuck 'em.

174

I wonder if a paint could be developed that would hurt one's eyes the way direct sunlight does.

175

Creeps generally vote for creeps.

176

Modern Dance leaves me dead-askance.

177

I write for my alter ego, wherever he is.

178

John Updike: **Self-Consciousness (Memoirs)**

Probably the most honest and best thing he ever wrote. A most excellent book.

179

I can stretch out the cocktail hour to one hour—one hour and fifteen minutes max.

After that, it's a question of diminishing returns.

180

If older writers had the energy to keep on writing, what certainties they would undo, what devotions they would discredit, what sentimentalisms they would annihilate, what myths they would dispel.

181

I'd like to think that everything that ever happened—all the kindnesses, wonders, injustices, sufferings, efforts—have somehow been **witnessed**…

and are **stored** and **recorded**.

182

Beware of letting a conniving and inept surgeon get his filthy hands on you.

183

Spare me, please, spare me one more time, spare me from those oh-have-read-everything-and-know-everything-and-so-full-of-allusive-brilliance writers who contribute to **The New York Review of Books**.

184

I don't understand it, can't explain it, grasp it, make sense of it, justify it…

but I still suspect that all times are simultaneous.

185

Some people playact to themselves.

186

If I were to be The Planetary Dictator, there's not much I could do about death…

but there **is** something I could do about pain.

187

There should be a drug that could take us back to those early times in all their intensity and immediacy,

and still be we.

188

The ranking of the Presidents, from FDR on:
(from a Joannidian perspective)

1. FDR
2. Barack Obama
3. Jimmy Carter
4. Harry S. Truman
5. Lyndon Johnson
6. Bill Clinton
7. John F. Kennedy
8. George Bush, the Elder
9. Gerald Ford
10. Dwight Eisenhower
11. Ronald Reagan
12. George Bush, the Younger
13. Richard Nixon

189

Barack Obama: I've never known a politician with so much **stamina**.

190

Making money can be such a bore and so deathly.

Now, **spending money** is quite another matter.

191

You have to forgive the momentary lapses of your friends.

192

Ex Cathedra 18, # 160

My God, I forgot all about Pearl Buck!

193

I like 24-hour restaurants.

194

Revisiting old haunts after many a year can be the densest kind of education.

195

I don't know which is more inane: American football or European soccer.

196

It's ok for H.L. Mencken to use big, fancy words; it's not ok for anyone else.

197

I just realized it: I'm older than most everybody else.

198

There are whores, and there are whores.

Those who do ads have to be the worst.

199

World Tourism: What an ugly phenomenon.

The ranking of Philosophers of the Modern Era:
(from a Joannidian perspective)

1. F.W. Nietzsche
2. David Hume
3. Bishop George Berkeley
4. Immanuel Kant
5. Arthur Schopenhauer
6. F.H. Bradley
7. Ludwig Wittgenstein
8. G.E. Moore
9. Bertrand Russell
10. Georg Hegel

The ranking of the Ancients:
(ditto)

1. Protagoras
2. Democritus
3. Heraclitus
4. Epicurus
5. Epictetus
6. Cratylus
7. Anaxagoras
8. Plotinus
9. Socrates
10. Aristotle
11. Plato

202

The ranking of the Medievalists:
(ditto)

1. St. Augustine

2.

3.

December 1, 2011

Ex Cathedra

21st Encyclical

von Herrn Doktor Professor Peter Joannides

1

God damn it! something, but something, has to be always hurting.

2

Ex Cathedra 20, # 201

Honorable Mention: Thales—Anaximander—Anaximenes

(They should be positioned **after** Anaxagoras but **before** Plotinus.)

3

American Indians, with a strictly American accent, pining about their history and heritage:

Give me a break!

4

As long as there is a breath of life in me, there will always be the thought of payback time:

Cadet Captain MacDonald
~~Prof. Norman Malcolm~~
Lt. ---, U.S. Army, Norfolk, Virginia
Dr. James Gregg
Jonathan Galassi
Dr. Rahul Deshmukh

5

I love deltas, marshes, bogs, swamps, mangrove thickets.

6

I guess that worn and threadbare copy of **Trivia**—now 61 years old—is my most prized and dear bookish possession.

7

I guess I'll try to cut down on repetitions.

8

　　Perfection: the sun shining brightly, 72°, a slight breeze, 5,000 ft. above sea level.

9

I'm ready to reject or review every opinion I've ever had.

10

　　If I knew who those two Russian goons were who mercilessly beat that Russian journalist to a bloody pulp with iron rods, I would, had I the power, literally crucify them like they did Jesus Christ.

11

　　I can't stand any of those late-night comedic clowns on television, but if I absolutely had to make a choice, I guess I would go with David Letterman.

12

There are too many things going on out in the backyard: ants, wasps, flies, gnats, wayward cats, the temperature not just right…

I'm going to have to go inside.

13

The most beautiful English accent: it's a tossup between Paul Henreid and Louis Hayward.

14

How many times did I ride those elevators to the observation deck of the Empire State Building so that I could start **A NEW LIFE!**

15

Ex Cathedra 18, # 70

Add Montaigne to the list.

And at the end, the line: (Sort of like the philosopher's "sense datum.")

16

I really don't care what the Bible says…

about anything.

17

If Socrates had his Xanthippe, I've got my Nona.

No cascading downpour from above; only, **at times**, a torrent of criticism.

18

Memo to Nero:

Trying to restrict "contact" as a verb is about as lost a cause as curbing the unattached "hopefully."

19

I can hear the snotty critics now:

"He read Wolfe when he was 18, and never really got over it."

And the snots would of course be right, only not in the way they would mean it.

20

Talk about **rare birds**: a literary philosopher.

21

Time is to **The New Yorker** what **The New Yorker** is to **The New York Review of Books**.

22

Basketball is such a sloppy game.

23

CNN's Ali Velshi

A perfect example of Kierkegaard's other type of deranged man, without a spark of "inwardness," "a cunningly contrived walking stick in which a talking machine has been concealed."

24

What a **thirst** so many have to be known and admired by others.

25

A lot of religious people in the U.S.A. are fruitcakes; but then again a good many are quite decent folk.

26

Insects after you can be worse than men after you.

(And bacteria, even worse still.)

27

Some of those precious mansions and hideaways in **Architectural Digest** are downright boring.

28

If someone is a Republican, I know, **right there**, that there is a variance between us.

29

For someone who is a determinist, Ethics is reduced to Aesthetics.

30

I really got eviscerated after reading the letters of Patrick Leigh Fermor; but then, slowly, I still got back to Myself.

31

Ex Cathedra 20, # 126

Add to the last line: ", especially celebrities."

32

For some time now, I've realized that all my life I've been drinking that slop that passes for the genuine elixir of coffee, coffee at its best, coffee as it should be.
A daily occurrence, to be so shamelessly compromised.

(It came to me one day in an unassuming coffee shop in a small town in the State of Montana: a supernal cup of coffee, never matched before or since.)

I haven't done much about it owing to a mixture of wherewithal, impatience, busyness, and mainly laziness.

Maybe when I win the lottery, I will attend to this.

33

I always thought that Perry Como was at least as good as, if not better than, Frank Sinatra.

34

When you come right down to it, in **this** world, the most honorable and **transcendental** profession is that of physician, nurse, and medical staff.

35

I don't think I like Lenin, probably for a number of reasons, but one that comes to mind is what he did to the Romanoffs.

He could have handled it differently.

36

What would documentaries do without their music.

37

The other day I caught a documentary on Ulysses S. Grant/Robert E. Lee.

I found myself quite interested in the trials and turmoils of Ulysses S. Grant; and quite uninterested in the career of Robert E. Lee.

I finally switched off on Robert E. Lee.

38

Ex Cathedra 20, # 201

Honorable Mention: Parmenides

(He should be positioned **just before** Plotinus.)

39

Militant liberals are about as bad as ideologue conservatives.

Example: Rachel Maddow

40

    Slowly but surely, I am getting closer and closer to that famous dictum of Socrates.

41

No matter what the meal, no matter what the comestibles, sides, adjuncts, accoutrements…

I still have to have my **bread**.

42

I must be truly alienated from this culture.

I have been given to understand that there was and is quite a craze to own and lay claim to a Mustang.

And here I've all along been thinking, "What sort of dimwit would want to drive a Mustang?"

43

My maritime friend and picaresque traveling companion, Iannis Paksimadis, hated uniforms. Any uniform.

I think about him and his antipathy quite a lot.

44

There is nothing quite like a good Western Omelet.

45

When I was a kid, there was this excited and futuristic, almost mystical, talk about **A FLYING WING!**

Now there really is one.

46

Even with the kind of minimal and staged exposure you get on TV, it's sometimes quite easy to tell who's the good guy and who's the bad one.

47

Memo to astronomers and cosmologists:

The World is far vaster than the Universe.

48

I feel contempt and disrespect for writers who unscientifically destroy all their puerile and adolescent and antecedent scribblings so as to appear oh so fully-grown and newly-hatched.

49

Accidents, so many **accidents**, now and back through time: rail, maritime, industrial, automobile, aircraft, mining, fires, explosions, stampedes…

Disasters, so many **disasters**, now and back through time: floods, earthquakes, typhoons, tornadoes, cyclones, droughts, epidemics, tsunamis, heat waves, avalanches, mudslides…

Like winning the lottery in reverse.

50

Some of those porno films are great.

But there has to be a story.

A story, a story, there has to be a story!

51

Maybe Michael Bloomberg should run for President.

52

 # 13

Christopher Lee and Ronald Colman are also in the running.

53

Given all my railings and contempt and dismissal of fiction, I suppose it's only fair to ask:

What about Wolfe and Verne and Jonathan Swift and Dostoyevsky and Kazantzakis and H. Rider Haggard and Rex Stout?

(As well as Salinger and Orwell and Hermann Hesse and Stefan Zweig and Daniel Defoe and A. Conan Doyle and Kafka and Simenon and Eric Ambler and Jhumpa Lahiri and a host of others?)

Ah! but that's a **different** kind of fiction.

54

Immanuel Kant: a terrible writer; a great philosopher.

55

Senator Dick Durbin of Illinois is one of the good guys.

56

I do a lot of **a priori** critiquing, can't stand-ing, hating, praising, acclaiming…

57

When you come right down to it, I was closer to Billy Batson/Captain Marvel than I ever was to Superman.

58

I liked Reagan more as an actor than as a President.

59

I seem to have a predisposition to like Italy, and things Italian.

60

It's getting to the point where I positively **DETEST** ads—just about any ad.

61

I wonder if people realize that Fred Astaire was a most soothing and delightful singer as well as the greatest dancer.

62

Oh how many have now gone from the locker room of the Jacksonville Y.M.C.A.

63

Can you imagine the difficulty of going from the obscene planetary population of 7,000,000,000 to the optimum figure of 300,000,000, each individual radiantly healthy and aware, and living the equivalent life of a multimillionaire.

64

I realize that Woody Allen was one of Sid Caesar's writers; but I still can't stand him.

65

Yesterday, while watching a film about Jimmy Carter, I caught Hendrik Hertzberg on television. Although I have read many of his commentaries in **The New Yorker**, I had never seen or heard him before. And I was pleasantly surprised. Somehow I thought he would be somewhat acerbic and egotistical, but he came across as limber and sophisticated.

When I become the planetary dictator, I want him to be my spokesman.

66

The severest taskmasters are dead ancestors.

67

I want to win the Nobel Prize for Literature and be the Planetary Dictator.

Nothing less.

68

I am often intimidated by engineers, inventors, and scientific innovators.

I sometimes wonder how important wordsmiths are in the general scheme of things.

69

Watching PBS and the History Channel is like going back to school again.

70

I especially liked the **beginning** of the first Superman movie.

71

Sometimes I think opera is just plain funny.

72

To reiterate (something I promised to try not to do):

Whatever is pre-photography,

Just doesn't seem to interest me.

73

Mike Huckabee: blabbermouth extraordinaire.

74

If I'm ever invited to debate, being a hopeless and terrible debater, I will let Bill Maher/Gore Vidal be my stand-in, with an assist from Hendrik Hertzberg.

75

Whiffs and fragments, from long ago,

come suddenly stealing into my consciousness,

and before I can begin to identify, remember,

just as suddenly, gone.

76

So often like a reel, a reel being played, tantalizingly played, backwards and forwards, re-backwards re-forwards, early New York days, 655 W. 177th Street, PS 173, the bicycle jaunts and the creek in downtown Hampton, the trip to India, old girlfriends and flirtations, the Alderman Library and Charlottesville, Fork Union terrors, the summers in Rhodos, the wanderings with Maryland, doctors and operations, the Bendix Diner and John wielding his meat cleaver, the Acropole, Pop and the World's Fair and the General Motors Futurama, Maya a baby, Maya a grown woman, Ninetta, Teruko, Connie, Esin, the vineyards in Crete, the obsession with the Magnum Opus, the handball nervousness and sleeplessness, on and on, Nona and slugging scotch in Baja, the time I slept outdoors waiting for the bus to Altamira, an endless array of startlements events, passing passing by, all jumbled re-jumbled, a reel, an ever insinuating defiant questioning reel, passing unyielding and not-to-be-denied by.

77

A moment of time, the ultimate **CONCRETE** reality, a mesh of age, mood, history, circumstance—

Hardly any writer, poet has even begun to capture it.

78

There are certain jokers and cretins on television that I simply **cannot** watch.

And **will** not watch.

79

What old people should keep in mind: they are the nonpareils and analogues of the flamboyant leaves of autumn.

80

It's the wrong people who become political leaders.

81

I like a car that purrs.

That purrs so smoothly that you can hardly hear it purr.

82

Some things I wrote are beginning to embarrass me.

83

Some players are astoundingly good in chess.

And others can instantly multiply 7-digit numbers.

So?

84

I sometimes wonder how we can have any new songs and melodies.

Aren't there just so many ways you can put notes together?

85

I remember how I was at that age.

How can I possibly blame another?

86

All my opinions, monomanias, enthusiasms, hatreds, dislikes, judgments, absorptions… are now becoming granulated pulverized re-worked re-issued and are **UTTERLY FLUID**.

87

To reiterate (something I promised to try not to do):

Bullfighting is disgusting.

88

There is nothing more morally reprehensible than torture.

89

On a typical day, I probably mutter the phrase "Fuck You!" at least twenty times.

90

Obama likes to talk and talk and talk and talk and talk…

He's probably one of the best Presidents we've ever had, but boy does he love to talk.

91

It really is a beautiful planet, with its seasons, its night and day, its semi-deserts, rain forests, plains and altiplanos, its coral reefs and wildflowers, its colors and profusion of wondrous animals, its monsoons and Arctic and Antarctic regions…

(As well as its scientists, inventors, researchers, creators…)

We had to go and fuck it all up.

92

4 A.M. at the Great Tokyo Fish Market, sometime in late 1960.

♪ No, no, they can't take that away from me ♫.

93

The Planet is s c r e a m i n g for a **Planetary Authority**.

94

The most common of my muttered "Fuck You" phrases is "Fuck You and Your Dog."

95

I might as well be living on a desert island, for all the genuine communication that takes place.

96

I've finally decided: God Must Exist. There has to be a **Witness** to the Truth.

97

Donald Trump: now, there's the real bottom of the barrel.

98

I don't have much use for people who have a valet.

99

Handball players and writers need to stick together.

100

To paraphrase Nietzsche:

The classic American: a great big **Head** perched on a thin little stalk of a body.

(As William Saroyan's Arab would say, "No Foundation.")

101

The thing that amuses me (and that I like) about Krystal restaurants is that before I can even pick up my napkins, condiments, utensils... the food has already preceded me to my table.

102

Teddy Roosevelt

It's hard for me to understand how, with all that gusto, bluster, and bravado, he remained a teetotaler.

103

Oh how clever are those who do those oh-so-clever ads.

104

Friends, Family, and Acquaintances vis-à-vis Celebrities

Not that they (necessarily) look like their counterparts, but, for me, (also) a certain strange and curious soulful affinity.

Roger Arias	Cornel Wilde
Stelios Elias	Dick Powell
Pop	Adolphe Menjou
Christoula	Jane Withers
Kiria Roussou	Merle Oberon
Alex Panas	Chevy Chase/Vincent Price

(continued)

105

Carl Feddeler	Charlton Heston
Doug Milne	Alexander Knox
Charlie McGhee	William Powell
Nona	Jean Arthur/Martha Stewart
Bob Bryan	Fred Astaire
Cleve Johnson	Robert Ryan
Petros Vrahimis	John Travolta (Smerdyakov)

106

Those Greek comedians: so quick with their wit and words, so lightning their thrust and riposte, so at one with their language and identity, so steeped in their Greekness.

107

What is it about an emergency that causes one to reinterpret, reconstitute, reappraise, recomprehend all and everything there is.

108

To reiterate (and I hope for the last time):

There's a lot of crud in Jacksonville, Florida.

109

I can't think of a city that is more violiny-trilly landlocked alien to me than Prague.

110

Languages can be translated, elucidated, explained, annotated, rendered one to another, and in great and painstaking detail, but in the end each one remains a private and irreducible cosmos unto itself.

111

Hume was strict-er and right-er, but Kant was profounder.

112

Some Great Films

Rashomon	**Invasion of the Body Snatchers**
It's a Wonderful Life	**Cast Away**
Casablanca	**It Happened One Night**
The African Queen	**The Best Years of Our Lives**
High Noon	**The Heiress**
You Can't Take It with You	**Citizen Kane**

113

The only way to travel is to wing it.

114

Descriptions of Death

I'm sort of partial to "Journey to 'The Great Beyond.'"

115

Odysseus and the Sirens

Oh how often have I forgotten to have myself lashed to the mast.

116

Sometimes something good happens, and we expect more of it.

But the fact is, it may very well be that only one time.

117

I would just love to see all the logistics systems interconnexions of the new Boeing 747-8 being interstitched and put together at the giant assembly plant in Everett, Washington.

118

You realize, of course, Petraki, that if you **were** to become the Planetary Dictator, the weight of the planet would probably crush you to death.

119

I stand in awe of grease monkeys.

120

Three Great Countries:

Italy, Greece, Brazil.

121

Despite all the looniness, coarseness, and crud, there's still an enormous fund of good will in the U.S.A.

122

Winning the lottery is my birthright.

123

I know of no one wiser than Nietzsche.

124

Bud Abbott, Lou Costello: "Who's on first?"

This has to be one of the most successful pieces of timing in the history of American comedy.

125

Jimmy Carter

I wish I hadn't ever heard or seen that "Malaise" speech.

126

A good by-word for my hero and mentor, Michel de Montaigne:

"I hardly know anything about anyone, except Myself."

127

My judgment is so much better these days, but I no longer have the energy to write about it.

128

Our experience is quite particular and delimited.

The intelligent man extrapolates as best he can.

129

In the end, that Cypriot accent is my home-going.

130

There's something likeable and eloquent about Pete Hamill.

131

Just think of it: to have the wherewithal and leisure to, night after different night, dine at the very best of each sort of ethnic restaurant in New York City.

Absolute bliss.

132

I never could understand why people say they can't sleep on a full stomach.

I can't sleep **without** a full stomach.

133

What more obscene: soldiers toasting, celebrating the destruction of the enemy ship, submarine, aircraft, city…

134

It's really too bad when friends of a lifetime have a falling-out.

135

I can sense animal food from fruit/vegetable food, **instantly**.

136

I remember, many years ago, King Idris of Libya did not wish to be disturbed while vacationing at Kamena Vourla.

And so the Greek police had to detour all traffic from the main highway to comply with the royal request.

137

The Bell P-39 Airacobra was the handsomest fighter plane ever built.

138

Flea markets are a wondrous study in structures. A plethora of structures-upon-within-structures.

I get drunk with felicity just strolling through a flea market.

139

I don't understand why Hume didn't end up a solipsist.

140

The photos in the photograph album might intimate a deeper and transcendent reality, but the stark and fearful and arresting reality is the here and now.

141

It's time I got over this thing with accents.

142

I'm surfeit with the phrase "The American Dream."

143

77

Jim Clancy, CNN anchor

I recently saw him on television here in Jacksonville. Out of place. He is inescapably tied to the cozy summer evenings in the cozy apartment in Rhodos, the international news, summer after cozy summer.

144

So much of modern American music is just so much **N O I S E** (and unappealing and discordant noise at that).

(Repetition, again.)

145

There's something tainted and unappealing about writers who take part in writers' events.

146

Fuck you and all your celebratory fireworks.

147

Inconsistency

I've always maintained that a nature program ought to be narrated by a male.

And yet, here is the soft and soothful voice of Meryl Streep suddenly interrupted by a croaky interloper.

148

I don't see why cooperation isn't better than competition.

149

So many things everybody seems to know about, I'm just beginning to know about.

150

Peter Joannides

A poor man's playboy.

151

My knowledge (such as it is) and interest in, from the most to the least (needless to say, from the vantage point of now):

>autobiography
>travel
>poetry: non-rhyming
>gastronomy
>documentaries
>history: post-photography
>ethnic music
>old American music

>(continued)

152

>biology/botany
>technology
>medicine/physiology
>sex
>physics
>chemistry
>sports
>movies
>philosophy
>history: pre-photography
>poetry: rhyming

>(continued)

153

politics
novels
concerts
opera
plays
art
modern American music
finance and economics

154

Fruits and vegetables are a wonderful adjunct to meat.

But that's all they are: an adjunct. Not the main thing.

155

 # 151–153

I forgot to include astronomy and astrology on my list.

Astronomy is to be placed just ahead of physics.

Astrology is to be placed in rock-bottom last place.

156

If there's anybody who needs psychoanalysis, it's "birders."

157

More or less new words for me, and so still uncomfortable words to use for me: "frisson," "tendentious," "panjandrum," "segue," "ersatz,"…

158

What more phony and ridiculous than turkey bacon.

Unless it's artificial flowers.

Or the fake flickering flames of the fake fireplace.

Or the plastic and indestructible Christmas tree newly-scented with the pine fragrance of the spray can bought at Wal-Mart.

Or, as Andy Rooney would say, non-alcoholic scotch.

159

Epicurus

What more sensible philosophy of life: the maximization of pleasure and the diminution of pain.

However, if choices have to be made and courses pursued, the moral imperative must be that the quest for pleasure has to play second fiddle to the concerns of pain.

160

Fuck Hemingway and all his bullfightings and his Pamplona runnings and his sailfishings and his war heroics and his precious understated brevities and his Key West posturings and all the rest of it...

161

When somebody takes a swipe at Wolfe, I take a swipe at the somebody.

162

Just think of all the things I've **not** had to do:

Be a city bus driver; be a toll collector; be a short order cook in a busy Waffle House restaurant; work in a coal mine; be a Presidential candidate and shake 10,000 hands and give 10,000 inane greetings in Iowa and New Hampshire; be a dentist; be a dental assistant; do ads and emote oh-so-heartfelt sincerities; be a waiter; be an entertainer and act the buffoon; be a grease monkey; work on dangerous construction sites; work in an office cubicle; tend to a convenience store for eight hours a day; be a superintendent of schools; be a car salesman; be any salesman; be a long-haul truck driver, hours and hours, and days, weeks, years; be a factory worker with one repetitive responsibility; be a receptionist and constantly smile; be a CEO and constantly worry; fight in wars for which I was too young and wars for which I was too old; be a shyster lawyer and make the worse appear the better cause; be a parasitical doctor; be a college president and constantly smile, ingratiate, and attend ceremonies; have dealings with thugs, thieves, scoundrels, and con-men; live in countries of crushing misery and poverty; live in the crushing megalopolitan sprawl of oversized cities…

What a fortunate and benefic-starred life.

163

In death there is no space, no left and right, no time, no before and after, no cause effect, no yes and no, no one and two and three, no same and other.

Courtesy of Immanuel Kant.

164

Now in these my later years, no one's standing has plummeted more than that of Ayn Rand.

165

Ex Cathedra 17, # 46

I forgot Mrs. Cheddi Jagan of Georgetown, Guyana.

166

Two of the sweetest men I have known:

Costas Ioannidis of Kremasti, Asia Minor
and
Pat Delapenha of Mandeville, Jamaica

167

Some other sweet men I have known:

Aristidis "Tzónson" ? of Limassol (?), Cyprus

Kyrios Antonis Akkidis of ?, Cyprus

Hector Pytharas of Dessye, Ethiopia

Father Mario Pezzotti of Marone, Italy and São Félix do Xingu, Para, Brazil

Gustavo Godoy of Jacksonville, Florida and Havana, Cuba

168

If I were to become The Planetary Dictator, Ian Wright would never do another Globe Trekker episode; Drs. James Gregg and Rahul Deshmukh would no longer practice medicine; and Jonathan Galassi would be totally removed from any editorial or publishing pursuits.

169

My mother used to say that most people who travel do so with a sack over their heads.

I'm beginning to think I may have been one of them, now with the illuminations of the History Channel, Burt Wolf's travelogues, Rick Steves' tourist guides, PBS documentaries, etc.

Sort of like an idiot, traveling with hardly any knowledge of the history, connections, reasons, customs, particulars of what is going on.

170

Traveling accomplishes not much more than "**miá trípa sto neró**." Things change, and change radically. All you get is a moment in the ever-newborn flux.

171

I find fiction (in all its forms: literature, film, drama, opera…) mostly sophomoric.

Unless it's really **good** fiction.

172

What in the world do people see in Willie Nelson!

A wailing, ululating cacophony yawped and caterwauled by a nasal-toned, straggly, unkempt, long-haired hippie.

173

In all this welter of conformity, I'm beginning to think extra well of Diogenes.

174

I miss ole Frank McGee of the **Today** show.

As well as Frank Reynolds and Walter Cronkite and John Chancellor.

175

There's no redress or substitute for the early years.

176

There's a lot to like about Christopher Hitchens.

177

I haven't really been put to the test.

About many things.

178

I'll even take Ann Coulter and O'Reilly over Rachel Maddow.

179

When someone criticizes Wolfe, I take it very personally.

180

Why would anyone need a job if we had Arthur C. Clarke's Duplicator Machines?

(Except, of course, those who would create **new** things.)

181

Would Clarke's Duplicator Machine be able to replicate itself?

182

It seems that so many of the good guys were assassinated.

183

Isn't it strange that I live in this particular time of automobiles and airplanes and computers and cell phones rather than in a world of horses and wagons and isolated villages?

That I could just as well have lived in the distant past and even the very distant past, or perhaps the future and the very distant future?

184

Isn't it strange that I was not born a zebra or an otter or an anchovy or a clam or a gnat?

185

There can be enormous guilt over a simple hesitation.

186

Try to think of everyone as they were when they were small children.

That way your judgment about some of them might not be so harsh.

187

I don't think I **particularly** want to visit Bhutan any longer.

188

In a way, it's kind of sad that everyone speaks English.

189

I never could see what T.S. Eliot saw in Ezra Pound.

190

There is something so insipid about so many Americans who travel abroad.

191

Oh God! how I would love to speak French, Spanish, Italian, Portuguese, Arabic, and Swahili.

192

It's hard for me to understand how anyone could not like Italy.

193

If it were up to me to obliterate one species on this Globe, it would have to be flies.

Even more so than mosquitoes, sharks, termites, rats, and dogs.

194

I forgot about roaches.

195

I'm beginning to realize that astronomy might be the only New Frontier.

196

It's sad sometimes when you can't read your own handwriting.

197

I think Ancient Greece is a bit of a bore; I like Modern Greece.

198

Between the pedants and the plebeians, I don't know where in hell I fit in.

199

I guess I didn't do too well in avoiding repetitions.

September 15, 2012

Ex Cathedra

22nd Encyclical

von Herrn Doktor Professor Peter Joannides

1

When an old and good friend dies, there is an especial void.

That proprietary understanding, outlook, perspective slightly askew, is no more.

2

It has taken me about 63 years to come out from under the haze of alcohol—a most wonderful, wonderful and unregretted haze, but still a haze.

3

I now understand Nero's dismay about traffic, and Hughes's dread of germs.

4

Olfactory pain can be as severe as any other.

Luckily, I have been mostly spared.

5

One of these days, the world will be run by scientists, not political ninnies and assholes.

6

I'm really tired of (American) Jewish intellectuals all entangled and ensnared in the coils of their Jewishness.

7

Saul Bellow winning the Nobel Prize is even worse than Toni Morrison winning it.

8

Physicists are sometimes full of it.

9

It's so hard for me to understand, **HATING** pain as much as I do, how anyone could wantonly inflict it on another.

10

I don't care how splendid the scenery, I simply cannot watch another Ian Wright episode.

11

I don't have anything against horses. They're just big and unwieldy (to me), and I've never had any special attachment.

12

An Interesting Question

My work is written in English.

However, there are many words, phrases, and even whole sentences written in a **Latinate** Greek (with footnoted English translations). (For example, the word "table" is rendered "**trapézi**.")

There are a few words, phrases, and even whole sentences written in the actual Greek alphabet itself.

How would a Greek translator indicate and handle this?

13

Why must nature always be photographed, painted, described, captured... Why can't it just be enjoyed.

14

I don't like some people. I can't give reasons. I just don't like them.

15

November 15, 2011

GOP contenders for President, 2012

Every single one is either a jerk or a creep or a looney, or a combination thereof.

16

I remember, many many years ago, somewhere in South Florida, I was part of a tourist group that stopped by a Seminole village for an entertainment.

There was a proud and handsome woman, an erect and almost regal woman, who with others had to perform for the assembled tourists.

I knew. She knew.

I lowered my eyes.

To this day, when I think about it, I **SQUIRM** with disgust.

17

I love the thought of eateries. All over the world, in Rio and Rome and Chicago and Hong Kong and Manila and Cairo…

People convivializing, gesturing, toasting, bantering, hubbubing, digging in…

The thought of it gives me immense pleasure.

18

TV Travel Hosts

(From the Best to the Worst)

Burt Wolf
Megan McCormick
Rudy Maxa
Art Wolfe (1st Place in Photography)
Rick Steves
Richard Bang
Joseph Rosendo
Ian Wright

19

It sickens me to see the patronizing Western "cosmopolite" join in the dance with the natives.

20

Globe Trekker Gals

I'd love to sleep with Justine Shapiro, but I'd rather be married to Megan McCormick.

21

When I look up at the starry constellations, I don't see bears, lions, swans, eagles, Big and Little Dippers, flying horses…

Just the wonder of the myriad stars.

22

I like light and buoyant, almost feathery, things: telephones, drinking glasses, bottles, silverware, jars and flagons…

Let others enjoy the heavy and the ponderous.

23

What can be more reprehensible than to make fun of someone for a physical ailment.

24

CNN's Gloria Borger

Now there's a lady who **REALLY ENJOYS** her work.

25

I sometimes wonder whether those who participate in debates, panels, committees, conventions, caucuses… may occasionally feel a bit of disrespect for themselves.

Or even a bit of self-loathing.

26

Ever since some celebrities came out of the woodwork after 40 or 50 years, I found myself getting into the habit, as with a time-lapse camera, of **aging** people, not only backwards, but also, more depressingly, **way forwards**.

27

Oh some reviewers for **The New York Times Book Review** and **The New York Review of Books**, oh how they just **OOOZE** with hubris.

28

I don't care whether someone is Jewish or not; what I'm tired of is all the hullabaloo about it.

29

In the long course of history, an individual briefly bobs up and down, bobs up for a few seconds (somewhere along a minuscule segment of the way), has a glimpse, and then bobs down, and is no more.

30

When I become The Planetary Dictator, Robert Reich will have a significantly high position in the pyramidal hierarchy.

31

Black Republicans: Surely, an oxymoron.

32

Friedrich Nietzsche

Despite his wisdom and indisputable genius, there are certain things he couldn't know.

Simply because he didn't live long enough.

33

What a beautiful passage from Zarathustra:

They call thee mine ape, thou foaming fool: but I call thee my grunting pig, I have divined thee well! But thy fools'-word injureth **me**, even when thou art right! And even if Zarathustra's word **were** a hundred times justified, thou woulds't ever—**do** wrong with my word!

Oh to how many things it can apply: musings of philosophers and poets, and modern physicists; skeptics, and organized atheists; quiet citizens, and organized patriots; reviewers, and reviewers; poets, and pedants; Nietzsche, and Ayn Rand; St. Francis of Assisi, and Billy Graham; Richard Pryor, and Chris Rock…

34

    I can't worry about people who have somehow mellowed with age; they're still responsible for the nutcases they were in their youth.

35

December 11, 2011

GOP contenders for President, 2012

    If I **had** to choose one of these alien harlequins, I guess it would have to be Jon Huntsman.

36

    I wonder if all those younger than I, realize how short-lived they're going to be.

37

I don't debate; I just dismiss.

38

 # 18

I'm beginning to think Joseph Rosendo is even worse than Ian Wright.

39

The difference between Ian Wright and Joseph Rosendo is the difference between a clown and a coxcomb.

40

Somehow, by the sheerest luck—near terrible accidents, near terrible embarrassments, near geographic imprisonments, illnesses, surgeries, economic entrapments, dangerous altercations, failed relationships—I have managed to come out of it unscathed.

41

Somehow, by the sheerest luck—the family born into, wife, daughter, son, profession, health, friendships, books and literature, handball, travel—I have managed to live a not uneventful life.

42

Oh the U.S. Navy Vets—what jaded travelers, what thousand ports and bars and cities—

    they've seen the world and are world-weary—

    they've seen and done it all!

43

18

I feel uneasy about relegating Rudy Maxa to third place.

I've decided that he and Megan McCormick will be co-sharers of second place.

44

December 28, 2011

GOP contenders for President, 2012

Mitt Romney

Never have I seen such **naked**, **salivating** ambition for the Presidency.

45

Bermuda: what a human mixture!

46

Being comfortably ensconced in a wheelchair while being wheeled around Hartsfield Airport is quite an experience.

47

For the Greek speaker who may be interested:

I **NEVER** use "**ótan**"; I **ALWAYS** use "**áma**."

48

I don't usually like to ride in taxicabs.

I don't like the sometimes awkward silences, or the awkward chit-chats; the sometimes rapacious and alien driver; the whole unnatural encapsulated bubble.

49

Solipsism is not only true; it's **laughingly** true.

50

Let's face it: I have an obsession with, and a weakness for, cheeses.

51

Alan Simpson of Wyoming: a straight and crusty good American.

52

I've been going over my old **Ex Cathedras**.

I'm appalled at all the repetitions.

My memory must be going.

I'm getting old.

53

If I have nothing new to say, maybe I should stop saying.

54

55

56

57

What's wrong with having an abiding interest in certain matters and themes, and coming back to them time and again?

58

Anyone who would have a TV blaring away 24/7, has to be a feather-brained bonehead.

59

The unfortunates and derelicts of society holding hastily scrawled placards at traffic intersections—"Will Work For Food," "Please Help, I'm Hungry," "Disabled VET And Homeless"—and engendering dismay, frustration, aversion of eyes, embarrassment, guilt, uncomfortableness...

Something that shouldn't ever have come to pass.

60

Only in America do people talk to one another via bumper stickers.

61

To be willing to give up one's life for a Righteous Cause.

This is so profoundly forbidding to me; and yet so profoundly estimable and captivating.

62

It's maddening not to be able to understand French- and Portuguese-speaking Africans.

63

I can get into such rages—become utterly livid—when things don't go my way.

Even a simple thing like some inanimate object slipping out of my fingers and rolling hiding in some invisible crevice (shades of Benchley).

Maybe it won't do for me to be The Planetary Dictator.

64

Those who do ads are greater whores than real whores.

65

I'm always on the **verge** of some overwhelming and revolutionary awareness, but always on the verge, never at a consummation.

66

Ex Cathedra Booklets

6th, 7th, and 8th Encyclicals

Collectors' Items

Only one of each remaining.

67

I would like to have been a roving British emissary sent to all the far-flung outposts of Empire—

in

1 9 1 0.

68

I feel such disgust for those who patronize the natives, because I used to do it myself.

69

What I like about the reviews in **The New York Times Book Review** is that they're short.

70

I don't mind The Big Bang, provided it is subservient to The Steady State.

71

Sex is hardly the most important thing, but it seems to override everything else.

72

Tag line for Rodney Dangerfield: "I don't get no respect."

Good tag line for Peter Joannides: "Whaddou **I** know?"

73

In these days, to be unfamous and uncontroversial is probably good for your health.

74

Despite the ugliness of the accent, in an emergency I'd rather be with New Yorkers than anyone else.

75

Restaurants that announce what they're famous for are about as bad as places that announce that they're historic.

76

When I begin eating (dining), I want no hiatus in the culinary flow.

77

Aside from his little TV baubles and gems, Andy Rooney was probably one of the best **writers** of recent times.

78

I don't like the word "iconic." I find it sounding self-important, groupie, and full of cant.

79

How much cleaner a world it would be without cats and dogs.

80

My five senses: see, hear, smell, taste, and feel.

It's the **feel** that makes for all the problems.

81

There's such a thing as being super-intelligent and second-rate.

82

Some of the fondest and dearest memories I have, have to do with food.

83

There'll be no **Collected Letters of Peter Joannides**.

It's a different world.

84

On a scale of 1 to 10, as far as actors go, Basil Rathbone (Sherlock Holmes) gets a 10.

85

You cannot will **sub specie aeterni** moments; they just occur.

86

I drink alcohol mainly for the effect.

Just about anything will do.

87

I wouldn't mind having the distinction of being the most contradictory writer that has ever been.

88

Ex Cathedra 21, # 43

I think Iannis Paksimadis is right. There's something about uniforms, any uniform…

89

The Amish:

What a half-ass situation.

90

What I learned from Robert Benchley and Max Beerbohm (not that I did as well as I could have) is to stick to my experience.

91

Every day I come across words I don't know the meaning of.

I can't even manage English well.

92

The enormous changes a baby undergoes as it makes its way from 0—5.

So too with codgers from 80—85.

93

A great heister is a great artist.

I can't bear it when a heist is unsuccessful.

94

Greek music at its best, and the Romances of Jules Verne: It's as if once entering these magic portals, I never again want to leave.

95

Trying to reason with denseheads is not far removed from trying to do so with animals.

96

Oh woe is me, I haven't been to Santorini!

97

It's the little delicate tips of asparagus…

98

It's the little delicate and slightly charred tentacles of **kalamarákia**…

99

No one belabors the obvious like sociologists.

100

Some Terribly Close Calls

Almost ran into my toddler daughter one day backing out of driveway.

Lost my toddler daughter for a terrifying minute in the surf at Jacksonville Beach.

Got hit so hard by an oncoming car as I pulled out onto a divided roadway that I was sent careening across the median and into the opposite shoulder in the face of opposing oncoming traffic (that mercifully wasn't there at the moment).

(continued)

101

Stalled a Piper Cub airplane soon after takeoff and plummeted nose-first into a providential clump of trees—where I and a startled passenger crawled out unscathed.

Flew back to Jacksonville from the Bahamas with Dave Scales and got caught in a storm, Dave's single-engine plane being bounced around like a ping-pong ball.

Fell asleep at the wheel on the autobahn for a few terrifying seconds during an all-night all-day drive.

(continued)

102

Almost had an altercation with a heavily-armed rebel soldier right in the midst of the coup in Upper Volta (Burkina Faso).

Came inchingly close to going over the side of a mountain road into the abyss of a cliff riding with my friend Costa Achillopulo in a jeep that slipped and slid and finally stopped in time (somewhere in Ethiopia).

Once in Macau, tried to illustrate the "double-your-bet" method to an acquaintance while playing roulette and came close to losing every last cent I had.

(continued)

103

Got caught in the surf and, panicking and flailing, kept being pulled farther and farther out. A lifeguard, who just happened to be on duty that weekend day, finally realized the situation and came rushing out to get me.

If I am to worship, then let it be at the Shrine of **Lady Luck**.

104

Backwaters are good places to live in.

105

You cannot will aesthetic epiphanies; they just occur.

106

Art Wolfe

The photography (with music) is so exquisite, you can almost forgive the paraphernalia and homilies.

107

What can be more uninteresting than a photographer showing us all the ins and outs of how he photographs.

108

Now that sex is out of the way…

109

If it weren't for all the astronaut photographs, articles, scientific unanimities, planetary predictions, explanations of eclipses and occultations, universal credence and persuasion…

I might still be a flat-earth believer.

110

My student Richard Weinstein committed suicide in August of 1994, leaving a note saying the world was going to hell.

I can't help thinking how many interesting things he's missed.

111

My mind is beginning to erase things.

Thank God I've got some notes.

112

Tom Brokaw

Former network anchor, author, historian, moralizer, literary critic, sociologist, Zeitgeist expert...

a man of parts.

113

Just as there is hard porn and soft porn.

So there is hard hubris and soft hubris.

Hard hubris: a goodly number of English professors; a goodly number of philosophy professors; Bill Cosby.

Soft hubris: Tom Brokaw.

114

Hal Crowther

There is such a thing as being a bit too proud of having the correct ideas.

115

Why would anybody have Florida lobster when he could have Maine lobster?

116

I can play that Albanian song **Kamarjere** with Eli Fara over and over and over and over and over again… and never tire.

117

A sudden and startling realization: I can no longer physically **run**.

118

All my life I've been involved with bugaboos, chimeras, apparitions, whimseys, shadowy wraiths, phantasmagorias, monomanias, queernesses, sentimentalisms, specious certitudes …

and never knew them for what they were.

119

Eating flamboyant tropical fruits in Central and South America is almost a mystical experience.

120

Coat of Arms—Peter Joannides:

aut Caesar aut nihil

121

Tigre music of Eritrea: I've been remiss and not given it its due.

It's right up there with Andean music, Greek music, Latin music, Indian music, the steel drums of Trinidad Tobago.

122

An isolated and I guess unrelated fact, but it still gives me pleasure to know it: Tabasco sauce is made by the McILHENNY Co. of Avery Island, Louisiana.

123

I must be lacking in some ways: I just don't get some of the jokes in **The New Yorker**.

124

The **Letters** of writers, including my own literary paragons and heroes, have always been, in some measure or other, disappointing.

Not so, those of Thomas Wolfe.

125

My impression is that Wittgenstein, although a penetrating and original thinker, was also somewhat of a showman.

126

My God! A President who doesn't drink.

What are we in for.

127

I don't want to be beholden to **anyone** or **anything**.

That's the whole point of the lottery.

128

Old black-and-white films of old square motor cars and people moving hurriedly and staccato-like along bygone streets and thoroughfares…

They're all dead, long dead, the old and the very young, every single one.

129

The knowledge of even the most knowledgeable is still terribly sketchy.

130

It's a very different world, and I'm having a hard time understanding and catching up.

131

At anytime, the roof can fall on your head.

132

Petros Epitropakis, Sophia Vembo, Fotis Polymeris, Nikos Gounaris, Jimmy Apostolou…the eagerly awaited Sunday afternoon broadcasts of old songs on Prodromidis (616 8th Ave.) radio—sweet and tender memories.

133

Many pundits and experts, although there is no question but that they are pundits and experts, nevertheless seem like **abstractions**.

134

I'm beginning to realize that being The Planetary Dictator would just be another taxing and unrelaxing job.

135

A sickening abomination: Trench warfare of WW I.

136

I wish I could have hung by the balls the politicos and generals who ordered the trench warfare, right in the middle of the ornate squares of Paris and Berlin.

137

Emendations and Changes of Mind

I am now prepared to admit that the Aurora Borealis is significantly beautiful in a way that firecrackers are definitely not. (In spite of being a closet purist.)

Recently, I had occasion to hear Perry Como and Frank Sinatra practically side-by-side. I must take back my remark that the former is equal to, if not better than, the latter.

138

Johnny Carson

I may be wrong, but I don't think all of that table-thumpin', falling-off-your-seat, uncontrollable laughter was genuine.

139

Ditto for "**Roasts**."

140

Architecture

I confess I'm more than tired of Parthenons, Louvres, Tuileries, Cathedrals, Castles, Temples, Alcazars…

141

The prospect of peeling the skin off a mango just about makes me forfeit the mango.

142

I didn't say that being The Planetary Dictator wouldn't be **rewarding**.

143

There's something about stricken and handicapped, compromised **children** that annihilates me.

144

There should be a strict disconnect between money and sport.

145

I can tell a jerk from a mile away.

146

There are more Ph.D.'s running around than you can shake a stick at.

147

What is it about some announcers of classical music with their unctuous undertaker voices.

148

Science-Fiction is not like the rest of fiction.

It is exempt from my diatribes.

At its best, it's as respectable as anything can be.

149

At the risk of repetition, here are some excellent films:

The Flight of the Phoenix
Naked Prey
The Incredible Shrinking Man
Drive a Crooked Road
The Gods Must Be Crazy

150

I remember them all: Joe Palooka and Knobby, "Daddy" Warbucks and Punjab and the Asp, Skeezix, The Little King, the chinless Gumps, Narda and Lothar, Hans und Fritz und Mama und der Captain, Pete the Tramp, Felix, Henry, Smokey Stover and "notary sojac!" and "foo!", Jiggs-and-Maggie, Pruneface, Moon Mullins and Kayo, Major Hoople and "Egad!", Downwind...

151

The only thing I'm **really** sorry about (and that even includes not winning the lottery) is that I'm not doing more traveling, my kind of traveling.

152

Ex Cathedra 19, # 45

Despite what I said about color- and black-and-white photos (and the artsy crowd), I'm **DEAD SET** against tampering with old black-and-white films.

153

If I'm to watch a documentary, I would much prefer an **English** narrator and host.

154

What is your favorite plant?

That's easy!

It's a tossup between a lavender wildflower against a backdrop of greenery,
                         and a cactus.

155

Oh how many mistakes I've made, both large and small, over the many years.

156

Wasn't it Fred Hoyle who said that in the Universe most intelligent beings are gaseous in nature—

That it's just too much bother and trouble to be a solid.

157

I wonder if you realize that even if you were given dictatorial powers, Planetary Dictatorial Powers, the job would be so **COMPLICATED** that it would send you screaming for cover.

158

#'s 100—103

    I forgot about the time (during the Charlottesville years) when, while driving and drinking and speeding with a carful of philosophy graduate students on the way to a party, we slid across a slippery main road onto a more or less flat field without hitting anyone or anything, and without rolling over.

159

    I can't forget, during a conversation with my friend and former student Herb Sussman when I was holding forth on the first thing I would do, had I the power, would be to destroy all nuclear weapons, his then saying, "Why destroy? We may need them to use against an errant comet or asteroid."

    And suddenly being struck with the correctness of his remark.

160

    More cant: "…sends a message…", "…bottom line…"

161

I'm just the reverse of Samson:

Before a haircut, I feel weak.

After a haircut, I become super-strong.

162

When Grand Tibetan Monks and Bhutanese Prime Ministers speak English with an American- or Oxford-derived accent, the whole mystique collapses.

163

Sometimes I have the hardest time finding an exact English equivalent for a Greek word.

There often doesn't seem to be one, and all one can do is resort to a circumlocution—and even that doesn't really do it.

Examples: **trómaksa!, remvázo, prósharos, kéfi, meraklís, grínia, mángas.**

164

I love the story of Flaubert who one afternoon put in, and the next afternoon took out, the very same comma.

165

After lunch, I want to do nothing whatever except go directly to bed.

166

No one so often hits the nail on the head like Logan Pearsall Smith.

167

I'll be honest with you: I think Shakespeare is somewhat of a bore.

168

I once fell in love with Laraine Day.

But then I recently googled her and learned she was a strict Mormon who never had a drink, never had a smoke, and wouldn't even consider a cup of coffee or tea.

I loved her, and she was a beautiful girl, but oh how messed up in the head.

169

I hate to be so severely dependent upon my car mechanic.

Utterly helpless without him.

170

Weltanschauung supersedes **Weltanschauung** in endless mad succession.

171

I've never been crazy about Kirk Douglas or Henry Fonda.

But I must admit I did like Kirk Douglas in **Strangers When We Meet**, and Henry Fonda in **Fail-Safe** and especially in **The Wrong Man**.

172

All around me, the world was changing in all sorts of significant and unprecedented ways...

And I had no idea.

173

I don't have a problem with astronomers; it's physicists that bother me.

174

As for economists and financiers, we might as well be talkin' Chinese.

175

"We always dream when sleeping. We just don't usually remember."

Although this is impossible to verify (and don't talk to me about brain events and correlations), it may very well be true.

176

 # 153

Unless it's a down-to-earth, working, blue-collar American.

177

It pleases me to know that God already knows the minutest genealogical details.

178

Some More Sacrilege

Frankly, I don't get it—all this exuberant hagiology about Joyce.

179

If you're going to tell about yourself, then tell **all** about yourself.

180

If certain inflated writers are going to pepper their work with cute little French phrases, I'll pepper mine with a little Latin and Modern Greek.

181

Religious **propositions** are either false or meaningless.

Religious **practices** can be barbaric, but also meaningful and beautiful.

182

I can tell you right now, **a priori**, that when a physicist or anyone else talks about a **God** particle, he's talking rank nonsense.

183

Some young people with their breathless enthusiasm, eagerness, and certainty make me sick.

184

Only a bona fide citified American, born and bred, can really get the rhythms, reactions, and descriptions of Archie Goodwin.

185

If, amidst the billions and billions of stars and galaxies, there are truly superior beings, vastly and incalculably superior...

then anything goes.

186

For a few milliseconds of a second—in parting and re-meeting— we get a flicker of a glimpse of the transcendental.

187

Confession

If I were comfortably ensconced on a chaise longue in my den and all I had to do to vote is push a button dangling inches away from my finger...

I would definitely push the button for Obama.

188

To really and thoroughly understand my work, you have to pretty much be me.

189

What an amalgam of personal memories, movies, literary idols and recurrent passages, dual languages and identities, evolving awarenesses, clichés and parrotings, film heroes and heroines, travels embedded in different spheres of personal maturations, sexual grippings and imaginings, Proustian auras, friends who know nothing of one another, irritations and illnesses, national and international events, patterns of societal changes, chimeras, confusions, all sorts of different measures of time...

all mixed and mishmashed together.

190

All these years I've been trying to win the lottery basically for myself—

now I want to win it for others.

191

"Why do people obey orders?"

This should be a subject of intense scrutiny.

192

How is it that Claude Rains, speaking with a definite English accent, can so well be believed to be a French officer?

193

If a movie were to have been made about Nero Wolfe, I know of no better would-have-been candidate than Sydney Greenstreet.

194

I wonder if Albert Schweitzer, in his reverence for all of life, would also have included mosquitoes, lice, fleas, parasitic nematodes, and chiggers.

195

Some snotty Brits all dug in and mouthing off on American Radio and TV (and I don't mean BBC News): I wish they'd just go home.

196

Opening Ceremony of the 2012 Olympics
(Aside from the Parade of Athletes)

Embarrassing to watch. All jazzy and glitzy and slick, absurd and irreverent, and sickeningly mawkish and theatrical all rolled in one.

Made me feel **UNCLEAN** all over.

197

Nothing adult even comes close to matching the wonders of early childhood.

198

I don't like anyone inadvertently even **touching** me in a swimming pool.

199

What good are stills when you have **motion** pictures.

200

I feel unfulfilled: I've not been to Torres del Paine.

www.ingramcontent.com/pod-product-compliance
Lightning Source LLC
Chambersburg PA
CBHW071257110426
42743CB00042B/1079